Africanizing African Legal Ethics

This book is a philosophical inquiry into indigenous African legal ethics, asking what is African about African legal ethics?

Taking us beyond a geographical understanding of Africa, the author argues for an African legal ethics that is distinct from non-African African legal ethics which are rooted in Euro-Western constructions. De-silencing African voices on African legal ethics this book decolonizes the prevailing wisdom on legal ethics and broadens our understanding of how law in Africa bears on ethics in Africa or, conversely, on how ethics bears on law in Africa.

This book will be of interest to scholars of African philosophy, philosophy of law, and legal ethics.

John Murungi is a Professor in the Department of Philosophy and Religious Studies at Towson University, USA.

Routledge Studies in African Philosophy

African Philosophy and the Otherness of Albinism
White Skin, Black Race
Elvis Imafidon

Africanizing African Legal Ethics
John Murungi

Africanizing African Legal Ethics

John Murungi

Routledge
Taylor & Francis Group
LONDON AND NEW YORK

First published 2020
by Routledge
2 Park Square, Milton Park, Abingdon, Oxon OX14 4RN

and by Routledge
52 Vanderbilt Avenue, New York, NY 10017

Routledge is an imprint of the Taylor & Francis Group, an informa business

British Library Cataloguing-in-Publication Data
A catalogue record for this book is available from the British Library

Library of Congress Cataloging-in-Publication Data
A catalog record has been requested for this book

ISBN: 978-0-367-42708-5 (hbk)
ISBN: 978-1-003-00708-1 (ebk)

Typeset in Sabon
by Wearset Ltd, Boldon, Tyne and Wear

Contents

Introduction

> *Wisdom is like a baobab tree; no one individual can embrace it.*
>
> African proverb

The study of legal ethics, whether African or non-African, ultimately takes us beyond the normal dos and don'ts in professional legal practice. It leads us to the study of ethics in general – a study of how one lives or ought to live as a human being. In this more basic study of legal ethics, neither lawyers nor their professors are privileged. It is a study that is fundamentally open to all human beings for it is about all of them. It is a study in which the being of every human being is at stake. Accordingly, an authentic African legal ethics, an ethics referred to herein as African African legal ethics, has being African on focus. Africanizing African legal ethics aims at ensuring that this ethics is properly and accurately focused. The legal ethics that prevails in Africa today is Euro-Western. It diverts Africans from themselves; hence, the need for an Africanizing ethics if this diversion is to be halted. Colonialism in Africa exemplified this project of diversion. Anti-colonialism sought to halt it. Today, colonialism has morphed into neocolonialism. Hence the continued relevance of the Africanization of African legal ethics.

At the dawn of postcolonial Africa, there was widespread belief and expectation that Africanization of governments would take place. European colonial legislators and high-level European colonial administrators would be replaced by Africans. Moreover, since Europeans viewed themselves as white and socialized Africans into viewing them as such, and viewed and socialized Africans into viewing themselves as black, it was assumed that white personnel would be replaced by black personnel. Apparently, Africanization called for a replacement of white legislators and high-level administrators with black legislators and high-level administrators. Clearly, race was a central feature in this process. This book opposes this concept of Africanization. It is pointed out that Africanization is precisely what it is: Africanization. It is not blackenization. Africans are not black. They are what they are: Africans. Consequently, what is at stake in the process of Africanizing African legal ethics is, indeed, Africanizing it and not blackening it. If Africanization is needed, it is because African legal ethics is still plagued by racism. It is yet to be what it ought to be. The process of deracialization is yet to come to an end. It is also a process that is preeminently ethical in that it seeks to reassert the human right of Africans to be African. In the reassertion of this right, African African legal ethics has a prominent role to play. It can properly and appropriately play this role by articulating what this right is. This articulation displays the intrinsic human worth that the African shares with fellow human beings. The arena of legal ethics is projected as one of the theaters that ought to display this worth.

Legal ethics whether African or non-African addresses the phenomenon of being human. Addressing the phenomenon of being human is more than a matter of knowledge. Fundamentally, it is a matter of wisdom. To the extent that most of modern legal education shuns wisdom and has reduced legal science to being nothing more than an epistemological concern, little is accomplished in delving into what is essential about legal ethics and about ethics in general. Africanizing African legal ethics involves paying closer attention to the essential role played by wisdom in constituting and disclosing this branch of ethics.

In human history, wisdom has not always been left out in legal education. But today, for the most part, it appears to have no place in it. It is not what attracts teachers or students to law school. It is the knowledge of law and the knowledge of its application that has been the center of attraction. Consequently, it may come across as diversionary when wisdom is broached in a reflection on legal ethics as it is taught in law schools. However farfetched it may appear, attention to wisdom may enrich our understanding of law, our understanding of legal ethics and, hopefully, inform legal practice. It may not be obvious, but a critique of conventional legal education may enrich legal education. Society stands to benefit from such a critique for the welfare of society depends on how legal education is understood. Taking legal ethics seriously as an integral feature of legal education (not only by requiring students to take a course on legal ethics) may enhance the well-being of society.

There is what is subject to wisdom and there is what is subject to knowledge. Seekers of wisdom are not necessarily seekers of knowledge, and seekers of knowledge are not necessarily seekers of wisdom. One may be a seeker of both but seeking will be blind if one mistakes one for the other. One who mistakes one for the other will miss out on the truth of both. Our age – an age that has increasingly fallen prey to the dictatorship of knowledge – has left little room for wisdom. This is the situation in which we find ourselves as we seek to understand African African legal ethics. There are those who expect nothing more than the knowledge of this ethics and expect to be presented with such knowledge by the author. I want to disabuse them of this expectation. What follows is not exclusively a matter of knowledge. It touches on wisdom. Wisdom cannot be put on a calabash and passed around for consumption by the hungry. This kind of passage is a matter of knowledge and not a matter of wisdom. In African cultures, if wisdom is ever transmitted, transmission takes the form of a proverb. In the presence of a proverb, there is no teacher and there is no student. One is left to oneself to make sense of the proverb. The African baobab proverb that opens this work permeates the entire work and seeks to preserve it in it. A proverb loses its sense if it ceases to be what it is. What is truly proverbial remains proverbial. What is essential about African African legal ethics is proverbial and must be understood accordingly. It appeals to the proverbial in those who seek to understand it. Elemental understanding is and remains proverbial. The proverbial has its own lucidity – proverbial lucidity.

A baobab tree is one of the oldest and among the most resilient of African trees. This tree is suggestive of what one can learn about African African legal ethics. To think about it is to think about Africa just as to think of African African legal ethics is to think about Africa. To think about it is to think of it as rooted in and as nourished by the African soil. Each of the branches of the baobab tree is a branch of the baobab trunk and the trunk itself is a trunk of the roots of the baobab tree. The roots of the baobab tree are rooted in and are nourished by African soil. Africans too are rooted and nourished in and by African soil and so is the African African law and African African ethics. This is the context in which one is to think about African African legal ethics.

By African soil, one is to understand African society and culture, both of which are to be understood in their multiplicity. Just as a baobab tree has branches, so does the African community. African African legal ethics is a branch of the African community. It is this community that nourishes it. The longevity and the resilience of the African baobab tree are analogous to the longevity and resilience of African African legal ethics. Respect for longevity in Africa is legendary. It is demonstrated by the respect that Africans have for their ancestors. Ancestors play a major role in the formation of the African sense of who they are. They are crucial for the existence of African African law and for the existence of African African ethics.

But it should not be forgotten that there is a colonialist lie that was once perpetrated by Euro-Westerners that Africans worship their ancestors and that they are resistant to change. Africans as is the case with other human beings have a complex relation with their ancestors. They keep what is worth preserving and leave behind or discard what is useless or what is an impediment to the present. What blocks the future is set aside. African culture is not a mummy or a fossil. It is a living culture. As Frantz Fanon reminds us, "Each generation must discover its mission, fulfil it or betray it, in relative opacity."[1] Each generation faces an inescapable ethical choice. African ancestrology is tapped to interpret the present, to critique the present, and to pave the way forward. If this is understood, one can grasp the trauma to which Africans were subjected during the slave and colonial eras – eras in which Africans were violently uprooted from their ancestral tradition and from their *homeland*. By being uprooted from their ancestral *homeland*, they became uprooted from themselves. There was an intrinsic connection between what they were and what their ancestral *homeland* was. The intimate link between them and their land was severed during the colonial regime. This severance was legitimized by the values of the Euro-Western colonizers. In his classical work on colonialism, Frantz Fanon has noted that,

> … every time the issue of Western values crops up, the colonized grow tense and their muscles seize up … Now it so happens that when the colonized hear a speech on Western values they draw their machete or at least check to make sure they are close to hand. The supremacy of white values is stated with such a violence, the victorious confrontation of these values with the lifestyle and beliefs of the colonized is so impregnated

> with aggressiveness, that as a counter measure the colonized rightly, make a mockery of them whenever they are mentioned.[2]

The above words were uttered during the heyday of the anti-colonial struggle in Africa. In postcolonial Africa, the horizon is relatively clear. It makes sense now to ask what values have replaced the hated Euro-Western values. We are asking about African African values. What has happened to the machetes that were close at hand when Euro-Western values were mentioned? Are they close at hand or have they been put away, sold, or been taken up by *Jua Kali*[3] industry and forged into different instruments and placed in local economy? Are the African African values that fueled anti-colonial struggle fueling postcolonial social existence or have the western colonial values resurfaced in new clothing? Concern with values is an ethical concern. Accordingly, to ask about the African African values that have replaced the hated Euro-Western values is to ask about African African ethics. I focus attention on legal ethics, and more particularly, on African African legal ethics to make the question and answer more manageable.

In writing about African African legal ethics, one should not only be mindful of the plurality of legal ethics in general. One should also be mindful of the plurality of African legal ethics. It is precisely for this reason that we speak of African African legal ethics. We do so to distinguish African African legal ethics from non-African African legal ethics. The distinction is not easy to make because different genres of legal ethics overlap. Otherwise, all would not fall into the category of legal ethics. Differently stated, no genre of legal ethics is closed off entirely from other genres of ethics. African African legal ethics is not an exception. Students of one genre of legal ethics can learn from students of another genre of legal ethics. What is true of legal ethics is equally true of law and of ethics. There is an overlap in conceptions of genres of law and an overlap in the genres of ethics.

The world in which we live today has reached a point where no regime of law is isolated from other regimes of law. Consequently, internationalizing of the understanding of law has increasingly become a necessity. With internationalization of understanding of law, there has emerged internalization of the understanding of legal ethics unless, of course, one accepts the separation of law from ethics. The separation may be societal or culture-specific. The jury is still out on what law is and what ethics is, and there appears to be no end in sight for jury deliberation in either case. Accordingly, the link between law and ethics remains problematic. To be sure, this process has not done way with the particularization of law or the particularization of ethics. Felix Frankfurter, a United States Supreme Court Justice once noted that,

> The law is what the lawyers are. And the law and the lawyers are what the law schools make them.

What he says is half of the truth. The other half of the truth is to be found in the answer to what makes law schools law schools. One possible answer is that it is the law and the lawyers that make law schools law schools. However, this answer is unsatisfactory. It is circular. And as such, it is an evasion of the answer. Law schools do not exist in a societal vacuum. Societies in which they exist make them what they are. If this is conceded, it would follow that it is society that makes law and lawyers what they are. In turn, law, lawyers, and law schools make societies what they are. They also give legitimacy to societies. Given the fact that human societies are not fungible, it would follow that different societies give rise to different law schools, different laws, and different lawyers. This scenario provides a basis for the grounding of the conception of legal ethics. Ultimately, legal ethics has a societal foundation. Given the diversity of human societies, an understanding of legal ethics must rest on its respective societal foundation. Hence, it is reasonable to speak of an African African conception of legal ethics – a conception that has its foundation in African society. It is pure obfuscation or nonsense to speak of legal ethics in itself – a legal ethics that is beyond the parameters of society. This obfuscation or nonsense is not without societal consequences. It opens the door for the possibility of societal imperialism – a situation in which a society imposes its will on another society. Legal ethics, in other words, improperly understood, can be of service to societal imperialism. In part, it is to alert one and to ward off the danger of societal imperialism that a case for African African legal ethics is being made. Law schools, law, and lawyers are not neutral. They serve specific societies. It is politically harmful to African law schools, lawyers, and African African legal ethics to buy into neutralism.

African African legal ethics: what is one to understand by this? Association of Africa with law and with ethics? Isn't Africa the home of tribes or the home of ethnic groups? Should one have in mind tribal or ethnic legal ethics? Is there law or ethics in African tribes or in African ethnic groups? Aren't African tribes or ethnic groups without law and without ethics? Aren't law or ethics primarily features of European modernity that have been introduced to Africa by the European missionaries of law and by the missionaries of ethics? Do Africans have a say in answering these questions or should they look up to non-Africans, especially to Euro-Westerners for answers? What or who determines the location of legal ethics? If Euro-Westerners stand out as the sources of the answers to these questions, it should not be a surprise because they have projected themselves as the global masters of the discourse on law and on the discourse on ethics. They have projected themselves as the missionaries of law and its rule and, if ethics is to have a place in this rule, it is reasonable to assume that they will also pose as missionaries of legal ethics. In modern history, Africans have borne the brunt of this missionary activity. Where missionary activity thrives, truth does not thrive. Missionaries profess to have a monopoly of truth and resist entering in an open dialogue on truth with those they perceive as their opponents. They are dogmatists. In speaking about African African legal ethics, one must be on guard against dogmatism.

In Euro-Western modernity, Africa has been projected as a lawless continent, as a continent without ethics which would make the concept of African African legal ethics empty and, hence, meaningless. Clearly, there have been and, perhaps, there still exist a European Africa and European Africans. Such an Africa has not been and is not an African Africa, and the European Africans have not been and are not African Africans. It is important to bear this distinction in mind and, precisely, it is for this reason that I qualify African legal ethics with the word "African" to set it apart from non-African African legal ethics.

Contrary to conventional belief, it is important to bear in mind that, from an African standpoint, there are no tribes in Africa. African tribes are inventions of Europeans. Without tribes there is no African tribal law and there is no African tribal legal ethics. Thus, tribal legal ethics exists only in Euro-Western imagination. Unfortunately, in modern African politics of self-reference, one finds millions of Africans who have embraced the absurd and preposterous tribal identity as their identity. Equally preposterous are Africans who seek to avoid tribal identity by adopting a modern or a cosmopolitan identity oblivious of the fact that these identities are essentially constructions of Euro-Westerners and are negations of indigenous African African identities.

In the period of history when Euro-Westerners constructed African tribal identities, they did not construct their own tribal identities. The implication was that they were a people without tribal identities and, given their evolutionary view of history, the implication is that they had evolved and transcended tribal identity. Tribal identity, apparently, is an identity reserved for backward and uncivilized people, which Euro-Westerners are not. Another failure to come to terms with indigenous African African identity is to refer to African identity as "tribal customary" identity which would make it possible to speak about the existence of "customary" law and, consequently, the existence of "customary" legal ethics. Here, the notion of "customariness" is contrasted with modern Euro-Western identity which allegedly has transcended customariness. One rarely if ever hears of Euro-Western "customary" identity which would imply the existence of Euro-Western "customary" law or Euro-Western "customary" ethics. Moreover, the term "customary" as understood in international law or as is understood in modern Euro-Western law, does not convey the negative implications when Euro-Westerners use it to refer to Africa to describe African "customary" law or African "customary" ethics. It refers to common or to usual practice within or among groups or entities. However, as generally understood by Euro-Westerners, African "customary" law refers to a law that is yet to count as fully "developed." African African conception of law and its attendant ethics is not a law in the Euro-Western evolutionary context. In part, it may be said that it comes into being as different from and in opposition to what Euro-Westerners have made of the African law and of its attendant ethics. African Africa law and its attendant ethics lead us to an indigenous African African identity on which African African legal ethics is to be grounded.

For the most part, today, what goes by the name of legal ethics is a Euro-Western construct. When Euro-Westerners write or speak about it, they have themselves as the audience. When they write or speak about legal ethics, there is no need to qualify it as European. It is taken for granted that it is. One who writes or speaks about African African legal ethics as if it were other than Euro-Western legal ethics faces a formidable task. One is pressured to prove that there is such an ethics. But for a Euro-Western writer or speaker who writes about legal ethics, such pressure does not exist. The existence of Euro-Western legal ethics is taken for granted. The Euro-Western writer or speaker does not even have to call it European since European legal ethics is *the* legal ethics. This legal ethics preempts writing or speaking about any other legal ethics simply by denying that there is any other legal ethics that one can write or speak about. Enormous pressure is exerted on the African to think and write specifically about the uniqueness of African legal ethics (African African legal ethics) and to stay away from gross generalization. Such pressure has grave consequences. It may lead to the silencing of the African since referential generalization is unavoidable. There is nothing inherently wrong with generalization if it is borne in mind that a generalization is what it is: a generalization. Generalization is inherent language. It is unjust to pressure Africans to bear the burden of being specific while shielding Euro-Westerners from bearing such a pressure. Specificity has limits. It could obscure what human beings have in common.

One of the missions of Euro-Westerners in colonial Africa was to silence the African African voice on legal ethics. To be sure, in their eyes, there was nothing to silence since indigenous African legal ethics did not exist. This silencing has continued in postcolonial Africa. To write or speak about African African legal ethics is to de-silence this silence and to bring into relief a renaissance of indigenous African African voice. To do so is to decolonize the prevailing voice of legal ethics. For Africans, at stake is the liberation of African African legal ethics, which calls for both the liberation of the law and for the liberation of ethics. This activity is not only foreign to Euro-Western legal ethicists; it is generally unrecognized and is dismissed by them as trivial or as inconsequential. African African legal ethicists are yet to break away from the spell of Euro-Western inspired legal ethics. They are yet to fully embrace the need for a liberationist legal ethics – an ethics that would have an African African footing. Most of them are parasitic to Euro-Western legal ethicists and are likely to regard liberationist legal ethics as an unwelcome distraction from legal education and from legal practice.

Scholars who have written or spoken about legal ethics have had in mind fellow legal ethics scholars, legal ethics professors, law students, or practicing lawyers. They are at home in a cage populated primarily by this audience. Euro-Western conversation on legal ethics is held hostage in this cage. The conversation is privatized or monopolized by the population in this cage. In what follows, what is said about African African legal ethics is intended to contribute to the freeing of the conversation on legal ethics from this cage and to releasing it into the public arena where it essentially belongs. It should be anticipated that some inhabitants of this cage will put up a stiff resistance to this undertaking and will seek assistance from lawyers, administrators in law schools, and from the advocates of professional ethicists in non-legal professions. Although it is not explicitly obvious, ultimately, it is to the advantage of legal scholars, lawyers, and to those involved in legal education to contribute to the dismantling of the cage in which conversation on legal ethics is currently held hostage. Law school is no longer to be taken as the only home for conversation on legal ethics and neither are law journals, law reviews, nor other conventional sites for legal research and scholarship. Law school and these other sites are not to be construed as primarily the sites for the conversation on legal ethics. This conversation should take place primarily where it ought to take place: in society. Law and the ethics are essentially and ultimately societal matters. For Africans, it is the African African society that is to be the primary site for legal ethics, and those who seek to understand this ethics must do so in the context of African African society.

Lawyers and their clients do not live in a world isolated from everyone else. Neither lawyers nor their clients exist in a societal vacuum. They do not exist in a world that is separate from the world in which everyone else exists. Ultimately, knowledge of legal ethics is embedded in this larger world. Moreover, this larger world *essentially* legitimizes lawyering. Legal ethics exists and is intelligible in the context of general ethics – the ethics of this larger world. In what follows, what is said about African African legal ethics is intended to foster and nourish this awareness. It is a critique of in-house legal ethics theorizing (caged theorizing) that one finds in the bulk of existing legal ethics literature. At its peril, this in-house legal ethics theorizing ignores public legal ethics theorizing. A writer or speaker on African African legal ethics must do so in a way that does not legitimize caged theorizing and, to not do so, he or she must be guided by that from which legal ethics ultimately springs: African African society and culture.

In his book, *African Philosophy: Myth and Reality*, Paulin Hountondji asks a question that I believe is relevant to a reflection on African African legal ethics. The question he asks is whether the word "philosophy" when qualified by the word "African," must retain its habitual meaning, or whether the simple addition of an adjective necessarily changes the meaning of the substantive.[4] The same question can be asked of the expression "African African legal ethics." That is, must the expression "legal ethics" when qualified by the words "African African" retain its habitual meaning or must the simple addition of the double adjectives necessarily change the meaning of the substantive? The two questions are not mutually exclusive for, generally, ethics is viewed as a branch of philosophy. Hountondji's answer to the first question is "no." The substantive aspect of philosophy does not change and to the extent that ethics falls under philosophy the more the addition of the double adjectives "African African" does not change the substance of ethics. The adjective "African African" is nothing more than a geographical designation. Likewise, when applied to ethics, the adjective "legal" does not substantively change ethics.

One need not necessarily be bound to Hontoundji's position or to what he regards as the habitual way of speaking. It is not to be assumed that the "habitual" is necessarily correct. It may have to be rejected and replaced by a more accurate way of thinking. As a philosophical position, what he says requires philosophical scrutiny. It is the nature of philosophy not to embrace any position blindly. Every position is subject to scrutiny, and this includes what is presented as a philosophical position. Blindness and philosophy are like oil and water. Even if it is conceded that the adjectives "African African" in the expression "African African legal ethics" merely point to a geographical location of legal ethics, it is not to be assumed that the meaning of "geography" is self-evident. Geography is charged with human significance. How legal ethics bears on geography and, in our case, how it bears on African geography calls for decipherment. Adjectives are not outer coatings of nouns. Nouns are not their substances. Nouns do not lie under them or beneath them. Behind adjectives or beneath them there is nothing. Adjectives are locations for the manifestations of nouns. They bear the meanings of nouns.

When the expression "Africa African legal ethics" is taken up by philosophy, inevitably it is subject to philosophical hermeneutics and so is every word in this expression. It is subject to hermeneutics because what is expressed is not self-evident. The expression is made up of the three words: "African," "legal," and "ethics," and what each of these three words expresses calls for elucidation. When they are brought together in the expression "African African legal ethics" what being together means is likewise not self-evident. At the outset, to preempt a misunderstanding, I want to state that, ultimately, it is not my intention to finally make what is not self-evident self-evident. I intend to deepen and broaden the power of imagination in the domain of African African legal ethics and, hopefully, in other domains of legal ethics, and in ethics in general. In matters that are elemental, as is the case with our theme, what is not self-evident perennially remains as such.

It is unlikely that someone who is not a practicing lawyer or a law professor will be taken seriously when he or she speaks about legal ethics. Apparently, speaking about legal ethics is reserved for those who practice law, for those who teach law, and for law students. They are the ones who are directly involved in the world of legal practice and in legal education. They are the ones who have first-hand knowledge of the ethical problems that arise in legal practice. At times, professors of legal ethics in law schools focus attention on cases that have been decided to extract the gems of legal ethics – gems that they subject to critical analysis. They assume that they have the first and the last word in matters that pertain to legal ethics. For the most part, they consider those who are not members of the legal domain as intruders or as invaders who should be kept at bay. To do so effectively, they have professionalized legal education and legal practice. They have circumscribed legal practice. They have set up a perimeter around the legal profession and around legal education to ensure that no intruder breaches it to threaten the legal order within. They demand obedience from within and are ready to expel any insider who is doing or may be doing sabotage work from within. This is achieved through the establishment of codes and professional rules; and, of course, by helping determine who becomes a member of the legal profession. They call these codes and rules ethical (etiquette may be a more appropriate term of reference). Every lawyer is expected to be a sentry guarding the legal professional enclave.

Lawyers are strong supporters of the independence of the judiciary, for the judiciary itself is largely made up of lawyers and is supportive of the legal professional ethics and insist on autonomy or independence. Members of the judiciary rarely include non-lawyers. Apparently, the protection of this enclave is intended to preserve and enhance the integrity of law and it is assumed that lawyers are more qualified than other members of society to perform this duty. It is noteworthy that the independence of the judiciary is taken to be essential for the administration of justice. It is assumed by lawyers that, as lawyers, they are in a better position to do this than other members of society. But this is mostly another way for lawyers to protect themselves and to protect their profession. It is a way to secure and promote their personal and professional interests. Only lawyers are expected to be officers of the court, and hence are expected to render support to the judiciary. Members of the judiciary have established judicial ethics to regulate judicial service. As lawyers, they are subject to legal ethics. Judicial ethics is a part of legal ethics and, like the latter it is severed from general societal ethics.

It is remarkable that, like other lawyers, in their academic training, members of the judiciary do not distinguish themselves in the study of justice. They are trained in law, not in justice. The question of how those who are not students of justice are expected to be exclusive servants of justice or to distinguish themselves in the promotion of justice ought to be troublesome. It is not self-evident how they can protect what has not been an integral aspect of their education. The practice of law is the practice of law; it not the practice of justice, and the administration of law is not synonymous with the administration of justice. One ought to have knowledge of what one practices and one ought to have knowledge of what one administers. If lawyers are expected to be servants of justice, this should be reflected in their education. Moreover, professionalization of legal practice leads the professionalization of legal ethics which implies that only lawyers have exclusive authority over such ethics. This is the heritage of legal ethics that Africans have inherited from the Euro-West, and they have been making concerted effort to indigenize it. African legal ethicists have been taken on as junior partners by their Euro-Western counterparts. They are parasitic to their Euro-Western counterparts. Their legal ethics is essentially neocolonial. They are yet to embark on the process of decolonizing African legal ethics. This decolonizing process has no currency in Euro-Western legal ethics theorizing. Euro-Western scholars of legal ethics do not distinguish themselves in the process of decolonizing legal ethics. They are largely conservative legal ethicists – conservative in that they are mostly guardians of the status quo in their respective societies and, in Africa, most legal ethicists preserve the vestiges of colonialist legal thinking and colonialist practice. Were the decolonizing legal ethics process to take root in the Euro-West, Euro-Western legal ethicists would be challenging the colonizing legal ethics of Euro-Western societies. It would expose the complicity of Euro-Western legal ethicists in the colonization and in neo-colonization of Africans.

Generally, what is overlooked in the conventional lawyer's legal ethics, and perhaps what is unconsciously repressed or suppressed is a look into the ground upon which legal ethics rests. It is often forgotten that legal ethics is a branch of ethics and, as such, it cannot be fully understood unless ethics, of which it is a branch, is understood. After all, legal ethics is one of the branches of ethics and, to make sense of it, it must be understood in the light of the common mother from which all branches of legal emerge. Ethics is the mother of all branches of ethics. It is the baobab tree to which every branch of ethics is intrinsically connected. As understood today, legal ethics suffers from motherlessness. Administrators of law schools and professors of law should be charged with desertion for the neglect of the care of a parent. To be sure, one of the problems with the charge is that the prosecutor and the prosecuted are going to be one and the same: lawyers. Most likely, the charge will be summarily dismissed as frivolous and as a waste of taxpayer's money. Clearly, it is not in the interest of lawyers to indict and try themselves. Besides, the court is their private domain, and they will only let in those they want to let in, and it would appear masochistic for them to do what is apparently contrary to their interest.

It is not to be taken for granted that because lawyers are lawyers, they know what is best for themselves. Like the rest of us, they too are human, and ultimately, like the rest of us, they cannot fully grasp what constitutes their good without understanding what constitutes the human good. Ethics concerns what constitutes human good and it is this good that must be inescapably investigated by any and every properly understood legal ethics or, for that matter, by any other properly understood professional ethics.

What is said about African African legal ethics in what follows is primarily intended for those who have or ought to have an interest in law in Africa and how law in Africa bears on ethics in Africa or, conversely, on how ethics bears on law in Africa. Obviously, those involved in the legal profession in Africa and those who are involved in legal education in Africa are intended to be a part of the audience. However, it is not to be forgotten that law in Africa implicates all Africans and so does African ethics. Accordingly, every African has a stake in the connection between law and ethics. Today, this connection is not always recognized. At this age of professionalism – an age in which each profession pursues its own trajectory and in which professions have increasingly been disconnected from everyday life, disconcertion between professions and between professional life and everyday life are rarely noticed. Academic ethics and academic law have been construed in a way that institutionalizes the disconnect between the two academic areas. To this extent, in part what is said herein is a critique of the academy, at least in its modern European sense. It is argued that the disconnect is a construct produced by modern European concept-industry and then exported to Africa. It has had and continues to have a destructive effect on African concept-industry and on African life.

It must not be assumed that what is understood as law or as ethics in modern Euro-Western society and culture is identical with what is understood as law or as ethics in African society and culture. This Euro-Western assumption guided and still guides Europeans in their one-sided relationship with Africans. It was violently instituted during the colonial and apartheid eras. What is said hereby is intended to sensitize the audience to this imposition and to devise means of getting rid of it. To write or to think about African African legal ethics today is to undertake a project of accomplishing this task. The life of Africans is at stake. For an African, the study of African African legal ethics is a homecoming process. It is self-study. It is guided and results in an African theory of self. Ultimately, it is an anthropology that is centered on being African. This center does not exclude non-Africans. Both Af ricans and non-Africans have a common ontological bond that makes them all human beings. Whether African or non-African each truthful branch of legal ethics has an intrinsic link to this bond.

It is evident that human community is socially and culturally diverse. This diversity gives rise to diversity in the conception of law, in the conception of ethics, and in the conception of legal ethics. However, in spite of diversity, the human community remains unified as a human community. Accordingly, in spite of diversity in the conception of law, in the conception of ethics, and in the conception of legal ethics, there is an underlying unity which must be recognized if the concept of human community is to make sense. The recognition contributes to the regulation of the conception of law, conception of ethics, and conception of legal ethics. The regulation constitutes and sustains harmony in the human community and makes this community what it is. It would be absurd to expect a genuine African African legal ethics to be essentially different from any other genuine legal ethics. To be genuine, all legal ethics must have an essential link with all other legal ethics. It is such a link that allows for a meaningful critique of one's version of legal ethics and that allows a meaningful critique of legal ethics versions held by others.

There is an African saying in which it is stated that "a hand, however big, will never cover the sky." I am this hand and so is everyone else. It is a human hand. What I say about African African legal ethics is not intended to cover all that can be said about it. I do not profess to speak on behalf of every African African legal ethicist. No one can do so. Moreover, even if all African African legal ethicists were to try to cover the whole of African African legal ethics, much would remain uncovered. Similarly, if all human beings were to attempt to cover the whole sky, much of it would remain uncovered. As the African proverb says, "Wisdom is like a baobab tree; no one individual can embrace it." To believe otherwise would betray obtuseness. Knowing our limits evinces a degree of wisdom – a degree of wisdom that prevents us from uttering nonsense when we speak about African African legal ethics or when we speak about anything else. Recognizing personal or individual limitation to our knowledge and to our understanding provides room for others to contribute to knowledge and to understanding. The unknown and the un-understood haunts what is known and what is understood as a reminder that what is known is not fully known and that what is understood is not fully understood. This is the background from which we are to navigate the course of African African legal ethics. It is a navigation that at the same time constitutes this course.

An inquiry into what is African about African legal ethics forms the substance of this work. Although, for the most part, the inquiry is intended to be philosophical, it is of benefit not only to philosophers but also to non-philosophers. Because a philosopher is not necessarily a geographer, a philosophical inquiry into what is African about African legal ethics takes us beyond a geographical understanding of Africa. To this extent, Africa is subject not only to multiple interpretations, but also to multiple constructions. Current interpretations or constructions are not exhaustive. A horizon is open to more. Africa is horizonal. When it qualifies African legal ethics, it calls attention to unfinished projection or projections of this branch of ethics. Mogobe Ramose, a South African philosopher, has drawn attention to the Roman and Hellenic sources of the name "Africa" and maintains that Africans are to provide content and meaning to this name.[5] This book is intended to provide the content and the meaning he is calling for. However, it is important to bear in mind that the name "Africa" is not a canvas on which content and meaning are to be inscribed. The canvas is the content and meaning that is inscribed. It does not preexist the content or the meaning. It is not the *tabula rasa* of the classical empiricists such as David Hume on which sense impressions are registered and form the foundation of knowledge. The boundaries of Africa are the boundaries of its content and meaning. These boundaries are horizontal. They are open and must remain as such to do justice to Africa. What the Romans and the Greeks meant by Africa was Roman and Greek. What Africans mean by Africa is African. This book is a contribution to the African meaning of Africa and to the African meaning of being African. It is also a contribution to human self-understanding.

Notes

1 Frantz Fanon, *The Wretched of the Earth*, trans. Richard Philcox. New York: Grove Press, 2004, p. 145.
2 Ibid., p. 8.
3 *Jua Kali* industry is an industry where old or discarded metal objects are forged or fabricated to make new inexpensive objects such as axes, pangas, hammer auto parts, metal gates, windows, doors, etc. Jua is a Kiswahili that means sun. Kali is also a Kiswahili word that has several meanings and as used here it refers to the sun which is very hot. The objects are made on streets or in inexpensive sheds.
4 Paulin Hountondji, *African Philosophy: Myth and Reality*, trans. Henri Evans. Bloomington, IN: Indiana University Press, 2nd edn. 1996.
5 See, Mogobe Ramose, "I doubt therefore African Philosophy Exists," *South African Journal of Philosophy* 22/2: 113–27, 2003.

Chapter 1

Thinking about African African legal ethics

Is there an African way of thinking about legal ethics – a way of thinking that is different from other ways of thinking about legal ethics? If there is such thinking it would lead to and would be inspired by an African African legal ethics, or it would be based on such an ethics. Moreover, it should not be forgotten that, in thinking, but not only in thinking, human beings display who they are. If this is granted, thinking about African African legal ethics is as the theater where being African is constituted and disclosed. It is what one thinks about law, ethics, and their connection. Both law and ethics are about being human and so is there connection? The province of legal ethics is the province of being human. It is in this province where thinking about African African legal ethics is constituted and disclosed.

There are those who may be tempted to claim that there is only one universal way of thinking about legal ethics and that any other way is erroneous and a distraction. The seductiveness of this claim may rest on the belief that only one universal way of thinking makes it possible to bring thinking about legal ethics under the umbrella of reason. Reason, moreover, it is assumed, embodies the universality that is essential to the integrity of thinking. If this position on thinking about legal ethics is legitimate, one must avoid the error of confusing the parochial with the universal, or the contextual with the universal. Among us, there are those who either out of ignorance or out of ideological reasoning court this confusion. Moreover, if one were to engage in a universalistic thinking, one would be doing so from a specific context. Thinkers think in their contextuality. The affirmation of an African way of thinking about legal ethics inevitably embraces an African context, which itself should be understood as a context among other contexts. Moreover, it should not be forgotten that there is no context that has frozen boundaries. Every context is horizontal. It is in their contextuality that thinkers encounter each other. Thinking is native to the thinker. Otherwise, one becomes vulnerable to a spurious missionary activity launched by those who seek to illegitimately universalize their context.

To think is not necessarily to have an object in front of ourselves. If thinking inevitably calls for an object that is thought, how would we be able to think about ourselves? For, to think about ourselves we would have to be transformed into objects, thereby transforming us into what we are not. The thinker and the thought would merge into one, and there would be no thinking. Clearly, since we think about ourselves, we must turn to a thinking that dispenses with subject-object thinking, for it is only such a thinking that would be fruitful, but fruitful in an extraordinary sense. It is such a thinking we must turn to if we are to appropriately think about African African legal ethics. A thinker cannot divorce himself or herself from what is thought.

The claim that there is an African way of thinking about legal ethics (an African African way of thinking about legal ethics) does not preempt others from thinking about legal ethics in their own ways. In a sense, it serves as a prophylactic to prevent the harm that may arise from paternalistic thinking about legal ethics. The colonization of Africans has made them vulnerable to this paternalism. A part of the African African way of thinking about African African legal ethics entails decolonization of the thinking about African African legal ethics. Thinking this way sets this thinking apart from the thinking about African legal ethics that is dominant in the colonizer's world, in a neocolonial world. Let it not be forgotten that thinking about legal ethics is history-sensitive. The peoples who make up the human community are not all historically similarly situated. Their thinking is bound to differ. Much also depends on the societal and cultural context of the thinker. But it is not to be forgotten that contexts are not like lone stars in a cloudless night. They intersect with each other and this is increasingly becoming the case. To think today is to think inter-contextually. Cabral reminds us of an African saying, "Rice cooks only in a pot."[1] The human community has many pots and each sector of this community has its own pot where it cooks its own rice. What is not to be forgotten is that there is a pot of all these pots where each pot is located, where each pot is a human pot. A rice cooker who ignores this pot of pots will end up with uncooked or poorly cooked rice. Not to ignore this pot, the cooker does not have to abandon his or her own pot, for there is no pot outside the pots. It is a matter of recognizing that every cooker's pot jointly constitutes the pot of pots: many pots in one pot, or one pot in many pots.

As I was reflecting on what I want to say about African African legal ethics, I was reminded of the following nineteenth-century piece written in a United States paper regarding a common perception of the thinking that distinguished a lawyer:

> An old lady walked into a lawyer's office, lately, when the following conversation took place:
>
> "Squire, I called to see if you would like to take this boy and make a lawyer of him."
>
> "The boy appears rather young, ma'am. How old is he?"
>
> "Seven years, sir."
>
> "He is too young, decidedly too young. Have you older boys?"
>
> "Oh yes, sir, I have several: but we have concluded to make farmers of the others. I told my husband I thought this little fellow would make a first-rate lawyer, and so I called to see if you would take him."
>
> "No madam, he is too young yet to commence the study of a profession. But why do you think this body may better calculated for lawyer than your other sons? What are his particular qualifications?"
>
> "Why, do you see, sir, he is just seven years old today. When he was only five he would lie like the devil; when he got to be six, he was sassy and impudent as any crittur could be; and now he will steal everything he can lay his hands on. Now if he ain't fit for a lawyer, I would like to know what he would have to learn?"
>
> "Pretty well educated, I should think."
>
> – Fit for a lawyer
> Nebraska Adventurer 1835

I surmise that the conception of a lawyer the old lady has in mind is typical of how lawyers are viewed today in many parts of the world. One may think of this conception of lawyering as ethically offensive in that it ignores and dispenses with moral or ethical considerations in lawyering. But it could also be said that thinking of it as such does not matter in conventional lawyering and taking it seriously may undermine lawyering since in the Euro-West, it is conventionally believed that a lawyer is a lawyer and not a moralist or an ethicist. Or put differently, there are two types of moralities: the lawyer's and the non-lawyer's. Since, apparently, the lawyer and the non-lawyer live in the same world, conflict is likely to arise. Instead of seeking a resolution to this conflict, what the conventional lawyer often does is to ignore the non-lawyer's morality. He or she must anesthetize himself or herself. Such anesthetization is what constitutes conventional legal education not only in the Euro-West but also in some other territories of the world that have fallen prey to conventional Euro-West legal thinking. In this education, one is socialized to think like a lawyer. One must cultivate a legal mind – *the legal mind*. A reinforcement of this conventional Euro-Western formation of a legal mind was called to my attention in a quote by an American student of law.

> If you think that you can think about a thing, inextricably attached to something else, without thinking of the thing it is attached to, then you have a legal mind.[2]

It is not an exaggeration to point out that this quote is fashionable in American legal education and in every other legal education that is embedded in an adversarial legal thinking. It has a distinctive place in European legal education. To be sure there are notable exceptions that include a Marxist legal thinking that takes the class-nature of legal thinking seriously, and there is feminist legal thinking that exposes the patriarchal nature of legal thinking. There is also critical race theory that exposes the racist nature of legal thinking. If this type of legal education is brought up in an inquiry into African African legal ethics, what must be noted is that both American and European conventional approaches to legal education have played and still play a significant role in the formation of African legal education. They must be considered in laying down the foundation of African African legal education and in African African legal ethics in particular. A legal mind in the sense expressed above has been commodified and has been placed in the marketplace of legal education, and the principle of *caveat emptor* applies here. The designing of this marketplace and the selection of the commodities put into it is not wholly in the hands of Africans. If Africans do not keep their eyes open, they may end up buying what is self-harming. African African legal thinking is an existential necessity and not a luxury.

One cannot think about African African legal ethics meaningfully if one thinks about it from the standpoint of a Supernatural Sparrow. A Supernatural Sparrow defies earthly gravitation. It eternally flies without landing on earth. No one has ever seen it, and no one will ever see it. A human being is deprived of non-earthly eyes and, consequently, of non-earthly seeing. When one thinks about a Supernatural Sparrow, one engages in thinking that is purely imaginary – a thinking that does not bear fruit except in one's imagination. This is precisely the kind of thinking that is central in the thinking of a lawyer that is called to our attention by Powell. It is a thinking that is the staple diet for those who embrace objectivism in legal thinking or in thinking about legal ethics. An objectivist attempts to think from the standpoint of a Super Sparrow. As said above, it is a thinking that bears no real fruit. It thinks about what cannot be thought. To counter this kind of thinking, there are those who are tempted to turn to subjectivism. In subjectivism, one seeks to lock oneself within oneself but, in doing so, one inevitably recognizes the existence of others from whom one seeks to shield oneself. In other words, it is absurd to be a subjectivist. Moreover, succumbing to this temptation is counterproductive. One is held hostage to a binary thinking (objective-subjective thinking) – a thinking that is equally abstract and that is divorced from lived-thinking – the thinking that is presupposed by binary thinking. Lived-thinking is rooted in the lived-world. It is a primordial thinking in which the thinker and what is thought blend into each other and in which each gives birth to the other. It is also a thinking that is rooted in the lived-body – the body that is earthly.

Unlike a Super Sparrow, a real sparrow is encountered and seen with earthly eyes and, to be seen this way, it has to be earthly. Regardless of how high it flies or how fast it flies, inevitably it returns to the earthly existence which is its natural home. Real seeing is earthbound. One sees from earthly anchorage and sees what is earthbound. Like a real sparrow, a human being is earthbound. His or her seeing is equally earthbound. To be earthbound is to be bound significantly. The earth itself is significant. It is a sign. As earthbound, human beings too are significant. A sign calls for deciphering. In part, this is an activity of thinking. To properly undertake this activity, thinking must be viewed as significant. Thinking is a sign that calls for deciphering. In thinking of thinking this way, one is no longer a logician. One is no longer thinking in lifeless symbols. This is a thinking that dispenses with the symbols of logic. It is an animated thinking – what we have referred to as lived-thinking.

How one thinks about African African legal ethics matters. One cannot think about it from a vacuum or from a neutral standpoint, for such standpoint can only be occupied by the proverbial unsituated God who allegedly thinks simultaneously about everything from everywhere at the same time. Although perennially tempted to think from such a standpoint, human beings are eternally deprived of such possibility. The standpoint remains a product of human imagination and stays there. When taken as real, it exemplifies human hubris or ignorance and leads to absurd, tragic, and harmful consequences.

A legal mind, it is assumed, presents to us not only what a lawyer is but also what a lawyer takes to be law. Law, after all, is law as thought. The observation Powell calls attention to forms an insightful background to what I want to say about African African legal ethics. Legal ethics is what it is as it is thought. If one substitutes "an ethical mind" for "a legal mind," it can be said that if you can think about a thing inextricably attached to something else without thinking about the thing it is attached to, then you have "an ethical mind." Moreover, if one substitutes "Africa" for such "an ethical mind," it can be said that if you can think about a thing inextricably attached to something else without thinking about the thing it is attached to then you have "an Africa." In short, if you think you can think about African African legal ethics without thinking about what this ethics is inextricably attached to, you are thinking an absurdity. Such an ethics does not exist and, consequently, you are not thinking about anything. What African African legal ethics is inextricably attached to is African social/cultural historical existence.

Africa is more than a geographical territory, and what is more cannot be excluded when one is thinking about African African legal ethics. Social/cultural historical existence is intrinsically a part of what Africa is. To ensure that thinking about African African legal ethics is not extricated from what it cannot be extricated from, it must be guided by a thinking that is rooted in African social/cultural historical existence. It must emanate from it and dwell in it – not passively but as a constitutive agent of this existence.

It must open a social/cultural historical African path – the path from which and within which one must think about African legal ethics. In addition, thinking about African African legal ethics in this context cannot be cut off from thinking about legal ethics in non-African contexts of legal ethics. Conversely, thinking about legal ethics in non-African contexts cannot be cut off from thinking about legal ethics in an African context. Although these contexts are embedded in their respective social/cultural historical existence, all legal ethics contexts are inextricably intertwined. That is, ultimately and inevitably thinking in African African legal ethics must engage thinking in non-African legal ethics. Conversely, thinking in non-African legal ethics, ultimately and inevitably must engage the thinking that is emanating and guiding African legal ethics. This is necessitated by the kind of world we live in today. The gap between Africa and the rest of the world is increasingly narrowing. The gap that separates one legal ethics from others is increasingly narrowing. The narrowing is yet to be thought through, and one of the reasons that this is the case is that what is implied by this narrowing is still unfolding. There is also an unresolved problem in distinguishing false narrowing of the gap from true narrowing of the gap. The former narrowing is a planetary imposition of the thinking about legal ethics that is associated with the legal mind that Powell speaks about. The latter reflects a recognition of the diversity of the contexts of legal ethics and recognizes the inevitability of their interpenetration.

The belief that there is a mind that can think without thinking about that to which it is inextricably attached is deeply and broadly rooted in the Euro-Western cultural industry of ideas. In this industry, the concept of "mind" which also goes by the name "reason" has taken on a Euro-Western sense. Descartes's notion of a mind that is disengaged from everything else appears to have had a prominent place in modern Euro-Western thinking about thinking.[3] The modern Euro-Western substitution of reason for mind has led to a version of reason that shares the same attribute with a Euro-Western conception of mind. For centuries, "reason" has enjoyed a long reign in Euro-Western thinking. It has guided Euro-Western understanding of law as well as the Euro-Western understanding of ethics. In short, it has guided Euro-Western understanding of legal ethics. Saint Thomas – an important figure in Euro-Western jurisprudence – thinks of law as "nothing else than an ordinance of reason for the common good, made by him who has the care of the community and promulgated." Evidently, those without reason cannot have a conception of law and cannot on their own intelligently obey it. Among them, modern Euro-Westerners have included Africans. Africans are projected by modern Euro-Westerners not only as being furthest removed from reason but also as anti-reason. The exclusion was evident in the way that Euro-Westerners understood and treated Africans at the initial encounter with them. In colonized Africa, the common good Aquinas speaks about did not include the African good, and the community that was served by law did not include Africans. The common good that Euro-Westerners had in view was exclusively a European good, and the community they had in view was similarly an exclusively European community. The enslavement and colonization of Africans were a testament to such exclusion. It should not be forgotten that both the enslavement and the colonization of Africans were legal. This was the case not only regarding Africans but also regarding any other group of human beings who fell victim to the European colonial-imperial regime. In the eyes of Europeans, this regime was the regime of the ordinance of reason. It was not a violation of law. It stood for the rule of law. Apparently, in Euro-Western thinking, if one is to speak about legal ethics from the standpoint of reason, one must do so in the context of the European view of reason. Let us explore further what reason meant for Aquinas to get a deeper and broader sense of what was in store for Africans under the European regime of reason – a regime under which European conception of legal ethics fell. This must be taken into consideration to help us appreciate the struggle that must be waged to bring African African legal ethics into relief.

For Aquinas, reason is what distinguishes a human being from other beings. Strictly speaking, those without it are not human, at least, not fully human. This conception of reason appears to have been derived from Aristotle. It is he who claimed that man is a rational animal. However, it should not be assumed that what Aristotle meant by reason is what Aquinas meant or understood by reason. For centuries, the difference has been deeply buried beneath Euro-Western consciousness. Aristotle, it must be remembered, was not a Christian. When he flourished there was no Christianity. Jesus was yet to be born. Aquinas comes after Aristotle. He was a Christian theologian and, strictly speaking, his conception of reason was not derived from Aristotle or from the Hellenic industry of concepts. In Aquinas, the Hellenic conception of reason was

Christianized. Reason ceased to be Hellenic. In Christendom, a new sense of reason emerges. Reason was baptized. That is, Aquinas, as has been the case with many other Euro-Christian friends of reason, propagates a Christianized view of reason. The ordinance of reason that he uses to define law is, ultimately, a Judeo-Christian ordinance – an ordinance inscribed in man by God when he created him. Ultimately, it is a Divine Ordinance. In other words, reason is a divine spark placed in man by God. What is contrary to divine will is not an ordinance of reason and it has no force of law. Without this force, it is not law. Moreover, reason – the Divine spark placed in man, apparently – is assumed by Christians to be the same in all men, everywhere, and throughout history. There is no evidence that Aquinas and Christian theologians included Africans as a part of the men in whom God planted reason. In the eyes of Christian theologians, Africans were heathens and were deeply steeped in superstition. As such, there was no place in them for reason. Modern Christianized Euro-Westerners did not include Africans among rational beings. In their eyes, Africans were superstitious not only about themselves but also about the world in which they lived.

If law is taken as an ordinance of reason, an ethics that is subsumed under it, that is, if legal ethics is rational ethics, it is ultimately theological – theological in a Judeo-Christian sense. It is always the same everywhere. Therefore, it would be absurd to speak of African African legal ethics unless Africans become Christian converts. Clearly, this view of legal ethics would be unlike a conception of legal ethics that would arise in Aristotle's thinking. An Aristotelian legal ethics would be an ethics that would be grounded in the Hellenic conception of reason – a concept that is non-Christian, pre-Christian, and anti-Christian. Moreover, even if one were to embrace the Hellenic conception of reason, the landscape of reason would not necessarily include Africans that would be subsumed under such conception of reason. There would be no guarantee that there would be an African African legal ethics. There is no evidence that Aristotle included Africans among the men he claimed to be rational animals. Even if he had included them, colonizing and enslaving Europeans would object to their inclusion since, for them, Africans were not rational. Moreover, since for Aristotle, ethics was a matter of reason, by voiding Africans of reason, under their version of Aristotelianism, Euro-Westerners would exclude Africans from the fold of legal ethics. A people without reason, without law, and without ethics cannot have a sense of legal ethics. This is particularly the case if ethical life is taken to be an instantiation of rational life.

A smuggling of an ahistorical conception of reason in human affairs, such as the one that has prevailed in Euro-West, obfuscates historicism and cultural specificity of reason. When applied to law, such conception mystifies not only our understanding of law but also our understanding of legal ethics. If reason is to play a central role in the investigation of African African legal ethics, it must be a conception of reason that is grounded in the African socialcultural historical existence and not on what is exported to Africa. But an investigation of African African legal ethics need not be grounded in reason; and similarly an investigation of African ethics need not be grounded in reason. The belief that man is a rational animal is culture-specific. It did not exist in non-Hellenized or pre-Hellenized European culture if indeed there was such a culture (this is put hypothetically for Europeans are largely silent about their non-Hellenic, non-Christian culture. The belief that man is a rational animal is not inherently an African belief and neither is it inherent in any other culture. In Asian cultures, for example, one does not encounter the definition of man as a rational animal. The indigenous peoples of the Americas do not define a human being as a rational animal. The belief that man is a rational animal has been used by Euro-Westerners as a weapon in the war against other people throughout the world. If this conception has a global pull, such a pull is traceable to Euro-Western imperial humanism. Euro-Western imperialism is more than economic, or a political, or cultural phenomenon. It is a humanism constituted and propagated at the expense of non-Euro-Western peoples. Euro-Western notion of law and its attendant ethics has played a major role in this activity.

The claim that African African legal ethics does not rest on reason should not necessarily lead to the conclusion that African cultures or other non-European cultures that do not share this belief are irrational. The rational-irrational distinction is culture-specific. In African cultures, there is an African construction of what a human being is, and it can be expected that other non-European cultures have their own constructions of what a human being is. For Africans, what a human being is is not grounded in Hellenic or in Judeo-Christian anthropology. It has an African grounding. Accordingly, African African legal ethics, as is the case with every other legal ethics, is grounded in a construction of what it is to be a human. It is to the African understanding of what it is to be a human being that African African legal ethics ought to lead us. If there is a universal understanding of what it is to be human, this understanding cannot bypass the African or be imposed on the African. For the African, it must be local or native. Being human is local. Thinking about African African legal ethics is inextricably attached to African ontology – to the African ontology of the African. It should not be assumed that being rational is the foundation of this ontology or that African African legal ethics is an ethics that is grounded on reason. This should not lead to an erroneous conclusion that African human ontology has an irrational or pre-rational grounding, or that African African legal ethics rests on an irrational or pre-rational grounding. It should not be assumed that all men are by nature rational. Such a belief is culture-specific. It is one definition among other definitions of being human contrary to how being human is projected in Euro-Western anthropology.

In its European context, reason is inseparable from the European bag of tricks. There is what is magical about it. The European guardians of reason are magicians. It is used as resource for the construction of European identity and as a missile for attacking non-European peoples. Prior to the Hellenic influence on the people who call themselves Europeans, these people did not understand reason to be what distinguished human beings from other beings. There is no evidence that they thought of themselves as rational animals. Europeans appear to suffer from amnesia when it comes to their pre-Hellenic or non-Hellenic existence – amnesia that gives rise to a false impression that Europeans are heirs of the Greeks. They have repressed the consciousness of their mother. In colonized African they sought to extend this amnesia to Africans by making Africans believe that they too were motherless, and that their true mother was European who herself was a descendant of Hellenic mother. This European mother was the mother of their legal ethics. It was she and only she who could nourish their legal ethical consciousness and bring it to maturity both in themselves and in non-Europeans.

Today, the path leading to the proper thinking about African African legal ethics and, hence, to the African African ontology of being human necessarily calls for the engagement of decolonizing thinking. Doing so calls attention to the colonizing thinking that European colonizers sought to institutionalize and legitimize in colonial education. The best thinker in colonizing education was someone who excelled in memorizing what one was taught by European teachers or by their African surrogates. Teachers taught facts and students had to memorize them. The facts covered not only what today we refer to as physical or natural sciences and math but also to what we refer to as social sciences and the humanities. Indeed, there was no area of education that was outside the domain of facts. Students who excelled in doing so as evidenced in oral recitation or in written in exams were declared to be very intelligent or very clever. Both teachers and students were under the reign of the ideology of facts. They suffered from fact-fixation. In education, facts were sacred. The objective was to construct and produce a passive and uncritical mind or a passive mind. Education (as dissemination, accumulation, and storage of information) was the opium of the masses. Such a mind was reinforced in and by orthodox Christian education and in orthodox Islamic education – an education where beliefs were to be held by faith and were not to be challenged. Offering critical education was taken to be detrimental to the success of Christian and Islamic missionary activity. Likewise, colonizers correctly viewed critical education as detrimental to the goals of the colonizing process. In either case, the attempt was to develop a mind that was inextricably attached to what it could not be extracted from: from education that was dehumanizing the African. The colonization of Africans and the religious conquest of Africans as evidenced in Christian and in Islamic missionary activity aimed at subverting or depriving Africans of their worth as human beings under the pretext that this was not really taking place. Africans who were subject to Islamic education, likewise, found themselves beholden to uncritical reception of the Koran. God had spoken through Jesus or through Muhammad. Both law and ethics consisted of facts – facts that, so to speak were placed as it were in a calabash, and were to be dished out to students by their instructors. The European ordinance or command was the law and the Muslim Shari'a was the law. Legal ethics was either European legal ethics or Muslim legal ethics. Legal education in either case was essentially passive. It amounted to African students memorizing orders or commands and applying them according to preestablished procedures. This was typical of law courses including a course on legal ethics. Legal ethics was authored by non-Africans and imposed on Africans. It was inculcated in Africans by non-Africans that the African rule of legal ethics was not only not the rule of legal ethics but was in opposition to the real rule of law or to the real rule of legal ethics as pronounced by Euro-Westerners. In short, the concept of indigenous African African legal ethics was empty.

As indicated earlier, for the most part, in modern Euro-Western thinking, reason is synonymous with mind. The belief that mind can be extricated from what it cannot be extricated from is a product and legacy of modern Euro-Western doctrine of mind. This entity called mind is a product of European imagination which, in the course of European history, has come to be viewed as a real thing, perhaps more real than anything else.[4] Apparently, to be human, one must have it. It was conceived and given birth at a phase of Euro-Western thinking. It formally enters the history of Euro-Western thinking primarily in the thinking of René Descartes, one of the widely acknowledged founders of modern Euro-Western philosophy. To Descartes, thinking is an activity of a mind that exists apart from everything else. Moreover, if it is recalled that Descartes was a Christian, his conception of mind was essentially theological. Descartes agrees with Aquinas's affirmation that, at the moment of the creation of man, God planted mind (soul/reason) in man, and this mind was the light by which man could truly understand and truly know. Since some Christian theologians such as Saints Augustine and Thomas Aquinas were familiar with a concept of soul in Greek philosophy – an entity that allegedly was separate from the body – Descartes had a secondary source to reinforce his belief in the autonomy of mind. This fictitious entity was to become a central feature in Euro-Western thinking, and in the course of time, it entered the European imperial stream that sought to sweep away or sideline any obstacles in its path. It found its way not only into legal thinking but into philosophical thinking generally. Thinking about African African legal ethics requires that this fictitious entity be recognized and set aside. It is only in this way that its sense can be brought into relief. Thinking about African African legal ethics must be an engaged thinking by a mind that is not disconnected from what it thinks. It must be counter-Cartesian thinking. It must be rooted in the African sense of what it is to be human. Every legal theory, as is the case with every ethical theory, is ultimately a theory of what it is to be a human being. Law is a mirror of what a human being is and so is ethics. Clearly, this has not been and is not the message that is conveyed to Africans by European teachers of law or by European teachers of ethics. Today, even African teachers of law and African teachers of ethics, for the most part, distinguish themselves by imitating what their European counterparts are teaching. There is little that is African in the dominant conception of African legal ethics. The notion that thinking entails nothing more than making inferences leaves out thinking as what determines being human – a determination that must consider man's sociocultural historical existence. To think is to think sociocultural historically. Otherwise, one is not only not thinking, but one does not exist as a human being.

In the Euro-West, the notion of a mind that is extricated from what it cannot be extricated from has found a home in Euro-Western legal thinking and, by extension, has found a home in Euro-Western legal ethics. Neutralism, objectivism, and impartiality are essential categories in thinking about law and in thinking about ethics; in short, in thinking about legal ethics. For Euro-Westerners, reason embodies these categories. Rule of law – a rule that defines what law is, is intended to embody and exemplify these categories. Otherwise, law is not law. Apparently, in the light of these categories, it is absurd to think of an African African legal ethics that does not embody these categories. In other words, if one is to think truthfully about African legal ethics, such ethics cannot dispense with these categories. African African legal ethics must be the same as non-African legal ethics. That is, legal ethics is always legal ethics everywhere and accordingly, when legal ethics is qualified by the adjective 'African' nothing changes about the substantive dimension of legal ethics. On the contrary, what is claimed here is that this type of thinking obfuscates what is essential about African legal ethics. Characterizing legal ethics as 'African' substantially matters. The task – a very difficult task – is to show how this is the case. It is also a task that is not to be exclusively undertaken by those who are in the legal profession. Every African has a stake in determining what it is. To fully understand African African legal ethics calls for its de-professionalization or for placing it in the context of pre-professional African life.

Thinking that severs the lawyer's' ethics from general societal ethics and extricates legal ethics from what it cannot be extricated. The African African legal ethicist, as ought to be the case with every other legal ethicist, should avoid this pitfall. The pitfall obfuscates thinking about the nature of legal ethics. If it is granted that legal ethics is a branch of ethics, the nourishing and the flourishing of this branch of ethics, as would be the case with every other branch of ethics, depend on the nourishing and the flourishing of the tree of ethics. That is, the existence and the flourishing of any branch of ethics owe their existence in the existence and the flourishing of the tree of ethics. The latter's flourishing depends of the collaboration of the branches. Such collaboration requires that each branch not shut itself off from the other branches and from the tree that it is indeed open itself to other branches. It is true that we live in the age of specialization, and specialization has made significant contribution to knowledge. However, what has lagged is the knowledge of the whole. Advance in the knowledge of the particulars does not necessarily contribute to the advancement of the knowledge of the whole. The whole is more than a collection of the particulars. The advance of specialized knowledge should not obscure the deepening of the cost of amnesia from which most of us in our age suffer. To specialize is to break away from what cannot be broken away from, namely, the wholeness of our sociocultural being. We may try to pretend that it is not the case, but specialization has given rise to a sense of alienation. Regardless of its success as a professional specialty, legal ethics may render us blind to the overall welfare of society. It is likely to end up as self-serving at the expense of society. It may desensitize us to societal needs – needs that when met contribute societal well-being. Legal ethics, ultimately, serves societal well-being, not just the well-being of the lawyer or the well-being of the lawyer's client. A lawyer has his or her society as his or her client. It is in this context that African African legal ethics is to be constituted and understood. Neither the understanding of law nor the understanding of ethics can fully make sense if that from which they emerge is not understood. Similarly, the linkage between law and ethics cannot be fully understood outside the societal context. Ultimately, legal theory is a social theory just as ethical theory is a social theory. The linkage of legal theory and ethical theory rests on social theory. African African legal ethics is an ethics of African society. It receives its nourishment from African social theory, from African society.

What is overlooked in the lawyer's legal ethics, and perhaps what is unconsciously repressed or suppressed is a look into the ground upon which legal ethics rests. It is often forgotten that legal ethics is a branch of ethics and, as such, it cannot be understood fully unless ethics, that of which it is a branch is understood. After all, legal ethics is one of the branches of ethics and to make sense of it, it must be understood in the light of the common mother from which all branches of law emerge. Ethics is the mother of all branches of ethics. It is the tree to which every branch of ethics is intrinsically joined. Legal ethics, today, suffers from motherlessness. Administrators of law schools and professors of law should be charged with desertion for the neglect of the care of a parent. To be sure, one of the problems with the charge is that the prosecutor and the prosecuted are going to be one and the same: lawyers. Most likely, the charge will be summarily dismissed as frivolous and as a waste of taxpayer's money. Clearly, it is not in the interest of lawyers to indict and try themselves. Besides the court is their private domain and they will only let in those they want to let in, and it would appear masochistic for them to do what is apparently contrary to their interest. It is not to be taken for granted that because lawyers are lawyers, they know what is best for them. Like the rest of us, they too are human and, ultimately, like the rest of us, they cannot fully grasp what constitutes their good without understanding what constitutes the human good. Ethics concerns what constitutes human good and it is this good that must be inescapably investigated by any and every properly understood legal ethics or, for that matter, any other properly understood professional or non-professional ethics. Legal thinking cannot adequately be thought without thinking about the societal good that drives it and that to which it ultimately aims.

For the most part, African African legal ethics is foreign not only to Africans but also to non-Africans. Accordingly, there is what an African can learn about it as is the case with a non-African. In other words, an African should not assume that he or she has advantage over a non-African when it comes to learning about African African legal ethics. Such assumption is a product of ignorance and is an obstacle to learning what African legal ethics is. For the African, at stake in African African legal ethics is self-understanding and this is equally true of a non-African. Being African is not a mode of being that is placed on a calabash where an African need only stretch out his or her arm and grab it with his or her hands. It is not a mode of being placed in a calabash that can be handed out to a non-African. How a non-African can learn about himself or herself in African African legal ethics appears to defy common sense, for being a non-African he or she is not African. However, the belief that one is exhaustively the other of the other does not tell the entire story about one's being if only because, as a human being, one is a part of what the other is. I, too, seek to understand myself in writing about African African legal ethics. Regarding myself, I am out of hand. It is by entering a dialogical relation with the other that one is what one is. Both law and ethics are dialogical. They are characteristic of intra-human relationships.

In its elemental sense, thinking is not what a human being does. It is not exclusively a cognitive or an intellectual activity. It is not an activity of the human mind. It is a social activity, a cultural activity in which a human being defines himself or herself. It is precisely this thinking that is in force in African African legal ethics and which is inescapably the force in every other thinking about legal ethics. It is also in this context that one must break away from the cage that is the law school. A liberated law school is a school where the teaching and the study of law is the teaching and the study of the society and culture in which the law school is located. A law school that takes itself seriously as an African school must be a school where one teaches or studies African society and African culture. It must where one teaches or is taught what it is to be an African in his or her sociocultural context. Law school is not a neutral place where law is taught or learned. In today's world it is inherently ideological in the broadest sense. One ignores this fact at one's risk. It is a place of ideological concealment. It calls for a dialectical practice where what is concealed is revealed

Hitherto, for the African, what has passed and what still passes as legal thinking or as legal education is an inculcation of Euro-Western social and cultural values. Euro-Western legal education takes on a missionary perspective. One cannot tell which is the greater threat to African social and cultural existence: Euro-Christian missionary activity or Euro-Western missionary activity embodied in Euro-Western legal education that has been institutionalized in Africa. Perhaps it is senseless to distinguish the two since both collaborate in a systematic destruction of African social and cultural existence. It is worth repeating that there is no thinking like a lawyer in a sociocultural vacuum. What is projected as a vacuum is a cover-up of ideological thinking – thinking that seeks to surreptitiously propagate specific sociocultural values. Thinking of legal ethics that ignores the sociocultural context is a thinking that contradicts itself. One's thinking about legal ethics bears the entire weight of one's sociocultural values. Among these values are the definitions of law and the definitions of ethics. Reflection on African African legal ethics takes us directly to African jurisprudence and to how this jurisprudence bears on African well-being. It is important to make a distinction between a lawyer's jurisprudence and a philosopher's jurisprudence. The two are not necessarily mutually exclusive. And how they are linked to each other remains to be explored. Even if the distinction is observed, there is still the problem of distinguishing an African philosopher's jurisprudence from a non-African philosopher's jurisprudence just as there is a problem in distinguishing an African lawyer's jurisprudence from a non-African lawyer's jurisprudence. To render these distinctions meaningful, it is important to elucidate what is meant by the word "African." As this is done, it is important to retain the awareness of the protean nature of this meaning – the open-ended meaning of this word.

Notes

1 Amílcar Cabral, *Unity and the Struggle*, trans. Michael Wolfers. New York: Monthly Review Press, 1979, p. 116.
2 Lawrence Rosen, *Law as Culture, An Invitation*. Princeton, NJ: Princeton University Press, 2006, p. xi.
3 See René Descartes, *Meditations on First Philosophy*. Indianapolis, IN: Hacket, 1993.
4 See generally G.W.F. Hegel's *Introduction to The History of Philosophy*, trans. Leo Rauch. Indianapolis, IN: Hackett Publishing Company, 1988.

Chapter 2

The African in African African legal ethics

What is African about African legal ethics? This question alerts us to multiple senses of African legal ethics. There is an African legal ethics that has been exported to Africa by non-Africans, and there is an African legal ethics that is indigenous to Africans. This indigenous ethics is what I refer to as African African legal ethics. In part, a truly African African legal ethics provides an answer to this question that I raise. Such an answer is difficult to identify because of the prevailing multiple senses of what it is to be African. Being African continues to be a contested mode of being. Consequently, what is African about African African legal ethics continues to be contested.

One of the major accomplishments of Europeans in modern history is the transformation of Africans into Blacks or into Negroes. This transformation was simultaneously accomplished by the transformation of Europeans by themselves into Whites. Today, it may appear incredible, but there was a time when there were neither Blacks nor Whites. Equally incredible today is the possibility that, in the future, there will be neither Blacks nor Whites. Africans are Africans and one must sharply distinguish African legal ethics from Black legal ethics. The latter is a Euro-Western product. It is internally linked to Euro-Western Black. The former is a product of Africans. Accordingly, by African legal ethics, one should not have in mind Black legal ethics. One should have in mind what one ought to have in mind: African legal ethics. Black legal ethics is a racist invention by racist people in a racist world. It has currency in a racist economy – an economy in which racism determines what can be said and what ought to be passed over in silence because it cannot be said. The African is African. He is not Black. The African speaks in an African voice. His discourse is not Black discourse.

An African who refers to himself or herself as Black suffers from dermatitis. Those who refer to Africans as Black suffer from diseased perception and most likely they too suffer from dermatitis. They have a pathological skin fixation – a fixation that they seek to impose on those who do not suffer from this disease. Appropriate dermatologists are still in short supply and full diagnosis remains out of hand. Accordingly, cure remains outstanding. African African legal ethics aims at remedying this situation. It aims at establishing African well-being. The determination of what this well-being is, is central to the objective of African African legal ethics. Fundamentally, this ethics seeks to bring into relief or constitutes what it is to be African – a being to which well-being is to be predicated. It divests the African of the Blackness into which he or she has been molded by people who call themselves White and from the ethics of Blackness – a mode of being that has been imposed on the Africans by the people who call themselves White.

The Black world and its Black citizens are largely a modern invention by Euro-Westerners who, in inventing this world, at the same time invented a White world and its White citizens. The citizens of the Black world are an invention of the citizens of the White world. It is a remarkable product of the genius of the Euro-Western man – the man Europeans invented and identified with and referred to as a White man. This man – a man who gave birth to himself and to his world, and at the same time gave birth to the Black man and to the Black world – is an unparalleled inventor. He is a pure magician. The transformation of the African man into a Black man and the transformation of the African world into a Black world was the work of this genius. These racist transformations form a dense dark cloud that obscures and blunts the emergence of African African legal ethics. African African legal ethics seeks to illuminate, scatter, and to obliterate this cloud. It is essentially anti-racist. It prepares the ground for the renaissance and the flourishing of non-racist humanity. It is one of the noble goals of African African legal ethics. Moreover, since racism has not been a feature of human history from time immemorial, African African legal ethics exists in a historical context. To fully appreciate it, one must take into consideration modern African history – a history that is inextricably bound to modern European history. There was history before the emergence of the White Man and the White World and there was history before the emergence of the Black Man and the Black World. In short, there were histories before these histories and there will be histories after these histories. African African legal ethics can play a major role in fostering this memory and in paving the way for the histories to come.

It is difficult to imagine a time when neither Africa nor Europe existed, but such a time did exist. At such a time, there were no Africans and there were no Europeans. If this is granted, it is also possible to imagine that a time will come when neither Africans nor Europeans will be in existence. The implication of these possibilities on what is understood as African African legal ethics should be obvious. This ethics has not existed from time immemorial and there is a possibility that at one time it will cease to exist. It is a transitory phenomenon and must be thought of as such. It is deprived of an eternal content. Its fixity is provisional.

As indicated above, racism has become a planetary regime. It is one of the forces that has fueled and shaped modern sensibility. It is one of the hermeneutical keys that one can use to open and to enrich the understanding of this sensibility. The so-called Age of Discovery or the Age of Exploration that begins in the fifteenth century brought about an encounter between Europeans and non-European peoples – peoples that Europeans regarded as inferior in the way they were and in the way they lived. They were deemed to be sub-human, pre-human, anti-human, or irrational. They were savages or primitives and deemed to be undeserving of human dignity or human rights. They were also deemed to be heathens – people who did not have knowledge of true God or the knowledge of true religion. They were treated the way they were thought to be. In the eyes of Europeans, among the depraved, Africans were the most depraved. The natives in the discovered New World were viewed as savages, but they were accorded nobility. They were taken to be Noble Savages. Africans were absolutely without nobility. They were quintessentially savage – the savages of the savages. They had no redeeming qualities. They were said to live in a Dark Continent and, to match their continent, they were dark. The continent had no sunlight. There was no sun. There was no moonlight. There was no moon. There was no starlight. There were no stars. No firelight. There was no fire. Africans were blind. They could not see. In darkness, how could one expect them to see? They might as well have had no eyes. They did not have eyes. The continent was so dark, its inhabitants so dark, that the only light that could pierce this darkness is the light from Europe. Light was provided by Europeans. Europe was the land of light and Europeans were the bearers of light. Being white was being light. Being light was being white. Law, as understood by Europeans, was a feature of this light and so was ethics. In short, from a European perspective, legal ethics was light, and it was this light that Europeans used to light up the African continent and that would provide Africans with the ability to see – the way they truly ought to see. This lighting of Africa was taken to be a civilizing mission. The European concept of law was central to this mission. It is Hegel who claimed that Africans had no consciousness of God or consciousness of law.[1] As such, they were not fully conscious of themselves as human beings. Apparently, without consciousness of law, legal ethics does not make sense, and without it, one is not conscious of oneself as a human being.

Having been thoroughly Christianized, Europeans were unable to resist embracing evangelical humanism. They became missionaries of humanism. Africa proved to be a fertile ground for paternalistic humanism. It should not come as a surprise that, when heard by Africans, European rhetoric on legal ethics has a racist undercurrent. European paternalistic humanism is a not a neutral paternalistic humanism. It is a racist paternalistic humanism. In it, neither law nor ethics is neutral. The combination of law and ethics does not alter this situation. From the European standpoint legal ethics was a civilizing agent in the discovered world, especially in the African Continent. Euro-Western legal ethics had the task of transforming Africans into human beings – to help them sever ties with the animal world, to uproot them from the jungle or from the bush. This task could be accomplished only by those who were already human, by those with a monopoly in the criteria for what it is to be human. It appeared to Europeans that they were the ones chosen to undertake this task. They were the chosen ones by their God – a God who had created them in His image and who had charged them with the global task of humanizing the non-human Other. This God of theirs is the Word. As His creatures and as created in His image, they too are of the Word and, derivatively, they are the Word. They are the sole custodians of the Word. The Word is language and language is the Word. With this as a partial background for speaking about legal ethics, let us turn to African legal ethics.

Like any other legal ethics, African African legal ethics is expressed in language. Accordingly, when speaking, writing, or thinking about it, inevitably, one is drawn into language. Language matters in what one says or seeks to say about it. It also a matter of how language is to be understood. I am writing about African

African legal ethics in English language – a Euro-Western language that is not my mother tongue. I am not writing in an African language. The medium of this writing has grave implications some of which are not within the range of my current consciousness. It should be kept in mind that a medium is not neutral. It is charged with the speaker's meaning. Language is significant. The sign that it is needs to be deciphered. Deciphering, moreover, is a matter of cultural orientation. By writing in English, I may unconsciously introduce some biases in my presentation of African African legal ethics. I may introduce a Euro-Western bias – a bias that may be deeply rooted in the unconscious. I am not entirely in command of what I say or of what I want to say. To this extent, I am open to leaning about what I am saying and to what I want to say. In an Introduction to *The Wretched of the Earth* by Frantz Fanon, Jean-Paul Sartre remarks:

> No so long ago the Earth numbered 2 billion inhabitants, i.e., 500 million men and 1.5 billion "natives". The first possessed the Word, the others borrowed it. In between, an array of corrupt kings, feudal lords, and a fake, fabricated bourgeoisie served as go-betweens. In the colonies, truth displayed its nakedness; the metropolises preferred it clothed; they had to get the "natives" to love them. Like mothers, of sorts. The European elite decided to fabricate a native elite; they selected adolescents, branded them with principles of Western culture on their fore heads with a red-hot iron, and gagged their mouths with sounds, pompous awkward words that twisted their tongues. After a short stay in the metropolis, they were sent home, fully doctored. These walking lies had nothing to say to their brothers; from Paris, London, and Amsterdam we yelled, "Parthenon! Fraternity!" and somewhere in Africa and Asia mouths echoed "... thenon!... nity!" It was a golden age.[2]

One of the issues that Africans face in speaking about ethics is whether when they speak about African African legal ethics, they are echoing Euro-Westerners or whether they are speaking originally; that is, from an African anchorage of language. The danger that besets me as I write about African legal ethics in English is that the African-ness of what I say may be in question. Most of what I say may convey an understanding of legal ethics that is embedded in English language. My paranoia rests on the fact that it is in the context of colonial experience that English language was introduced to me. What saves me from succumbing to this paranoia is the belief that my mother tongue has some shared meanings with English language just as it has with other languages. I will readily concede that it is difficult to distinguish with utter clarity what is and what is not held in common. Meanings, it should also not be forgotten, change and old meanings die out and new meanings come into being. Languages are not static. It would be erroneous to believe that what I say about African legal ethics is cast in granite. It evident that, here, I am writing about African African legal ethics in English language – a Euro-Western language that is not my mother tongue. I am walking on hot coals of meaning and my audience should take note of this. There exists a radical problem of communication here. I cannot guarantee that I am beyond uttering nonsense. One listens to what is being said here at one's risk. What I say about the "African" in the African African legal ethics is in the process of being constituted. What is said is not definitive.

Colonialism indoctrinated Africans into speaking with a European tongue but also into listening with a European ear. Giorgio Agamben, an Italian scholar, calls our attention thus:

> We should never tire of reflecting on the following fact: although there were and are, in every age and place societies whose customs appear to us to be barbaric, or anyway unacceptable, and more or less numerous human groups willing to question every rule, culture and tradition; although wholly criminal societies have existed and exist, moreover, and, after all, there is no norm or value whose legitimacy everyone could unanimously agree about, there nonetheless never is or never was any community, or society, or group that purely and simply chose to renounce language.[3]

In part, he is mistaken in the claim. What he takes as a fact is not entirely factual. The enslavement and colonialization of Africans were attempts at carrying out language cleansing – a process analogous to ethnic cleansing. It is an unchallengeable fact that when Africans were violently uprooted from Africa and transported to the Americas and to the Caribbean, they were stripped of their African languages. Their mother tongues today are European. Their African mother tongues were excised. What happened to Africans in

Africa happened to Africans in the Americas and in the Caribbean to a greater extent.

There is no language that exists in a cultural vacuum. Language is not only rooted in culture; it is also a cultural expression. European languages are deeply rooted in European cultures and are expressions of European cultures. Equally, African languages are rooted in African cultures and are expressions of African cultures. Speech on Euro-Western legal ethics is the flesh and expression of Euro-Western culture and, equally, speech on African legal ethics is to be viewed as the flesh and expression of African cultures; unless, of course, one assumes that African cultures do not exist as did the European colonizers and enslavers of Africans. As Fanon has reminded us:

> To speak means to be in a position to use certain syntax, to grasp the morphology of this or that language, bur it means above all to assume a culture, to support the weight of a civilization.[4]

The plurality of human languages reflects a plurality of meanings – meanings rooted in a plurality of cultures. The question I face – an inevitable question – is, how can I write about African African legal ethics in English language without intentionally or surreptitiously privileging the culture with which it is associated or with the culture that it embodies? How can I do so without doing so at the expense of African African culture? How can I express myself in language that is not my mother tongue without constituting myself as what I am not? Can an African be an African when he or she expresses himself or herself in a non-African language?

My use of English language is to be understood contextually. I am a product of British colonialism. If I were a product of French colonialism, chances are that French would be the language of my presentation, and if I were a product of Portuguese colonialism, Portuguese would be the language of my presentation. As Fanon has correctly pointed out,

> Every colonized people – in other words, every people in whose soul an inferiority complex has been created by the death and the burial of its local cultural originality – finds itself face to face with the language of the civilizing nation; that is, with the culture of the mother country. The colonized is elevated

> above his jungle status in proportion to his adoption of the mother country's cultural standards. He becomes white as he renounces his blackness, his jungle.[5]

The imposition of European language brought about in the course of colonialism brought about an imposition of Euro-Western culture on African culture. Accordingly, how an African construes and speaks about African African legal ethics is of fundamental concern. Highlighting this imposition is a part of its task. Setting aside this imposition leaves room to raise the question regarding the existence and presence of African African legal ethics. The question cannot make sense unless it is first determined what legal ethics is. To those who have already predetermined what legal ethics is, the question is not serious. It is a pseudo-question. However, the predetermination may not be warranted. The Euro-Western preemption of law and ethics in indigenous African societies and cultures calls for an investigation of the validity of this preemption. An investigation of African African legal ethics contributes to this investigation.

Is there an African African legal ethics? This question is most likely a child of an older question: "Is there an African philosophy?" This is particularly the case when the question is framed in a philosophical context. As indicated earlier, one of the respondents to the latter question is Paulin Hountondji – an African philosopher from Benin. His book *African Philosophy: Myth and Reality* details how treacherous this question can be especially if the answer put forth projects African philosophy as a unique philosophy that has nothing to do with what he regards as true philosophy – a philosophy that is universally the same everywhere and all the times. He takes the view that philosophy is like physics. Since physics (as a science) is the same everywhere at all times, philosophy, if it is to be true to itself, must equally be scientific. It must be universally the same everywhere. The only difference is the geographical location. In his eyes, what has hitherto passed as African philosophy is a bogus philosophy – a philosophy he calls "ethnophilosophy." It is a false philosophy created by Europeans for a European audience. True African philosophy – a philosophy that consists of scientific literature – is yet to come and it is to be created by African philosophers who think scientifically. Accordingly, in his eyes, if African legal ethics is to be viewed philosophically, what would distinguish African African legal ethics from other branches of legal ethics is the geographical location in which it is situated. Failure to recognize this would result in a bogus notion of African legal ethics. That is, true African African legal ethics is a legal ethics located in a geographical territory known as Africa. This branch of ethics is not a branch of ethno-philosophy. It is an error to assume that every African ethnic group has its own legal ethics.

Today, the question of whether there is an African philosophy appears to be philosophically dead. It may be of interest to the historian of African philosophy but not as a live issue in African philosophical thinking. Those who concern themselves with African philosophy are busy doing it. They are not worrying whether it does or does not exist. According to Hountondjian thinking, it appears that if African African legal ethics is to be taken as a genuine feature of genuine African philosophy, what must be avoided is reducing it to ethno-ethics. Instead of worrying whether it does or does not exist, those who concern themselves with it should be busy doing it. It would be absurd to make a special case for an African legal ethics since legal ethics is the same everywhere and always.

It is conceivable that a Hountondjian approach to philosophy and to its branches is driven by the pressure to universalize or to globalize thinking. However, this pressure must be subjected to critical scrutiny for it may be disastrous to philosophy and, hence, to its branches. What passes in the name of philosophy is not necessarily philosophical. How to separate what is necessarily philosophical from what is not is a perennial issue for philosophers. Accordingly, in determining whether existent or nonexistent, African African legal ethics is to be taken as an ongoing issue. Genuine philosophical issues are not to be handled in a hurry.

The question regarding the philosophical status of African African legal ethics cannot be intelligently understood or answered in a historical vacuum. The African of yesterday is not the African of today, and the African of today is not the African of tomorrow. The law of yesterday is not the law of today, and the law of today is not the law of tomorrow. The ethics of yesterday is not the ethics of today, and the ethics of today is not the ethics of tomorrow. If this historical trend is accurate, one can draw reasonable implications for the status of African African legal ethics. It appears to follow that the African African legal ethics of yesterday is not the African African legal ethics of today, and the African African legal ethics of today is not the African African legal ethics of tomorrow. On the other hand, if African African legal ethics is ahistorical; that is, if it does not change in the course of history, to ignore its ahistoricity does not appear reasonable. Clearly, at stake here is the philosophy of the history of legal ethics. One must make a case for the philosophy of history that is implied by either opinion should the term ethics be retained. African African legal ethics is sensitive to history. That is, it is not ahistorical. What the African African legal ethics reveals about the African is that the African is protean and as a human being, he or she embodies what is protean about being human. Being protean is not a monopoly of Africans. It is that to which every human being is subject. Again, what must not be forgotten is that indigenous African African legal ethics is not cast in stone. Changing belongs to it essentially. It is provisionally categorized. It is what it is contextually. The African in the African African legal ethics is an African who is in the process of endless constitution of what it is to be African. He or she is not to be found in genetic constitution or physical geography. African African legal ethics is one of the ways in which the identity of being African is constituted.

The existence or non-existence of African philosophy bears directly on the being of an African. Consequently, when African African legal ethics is taken up philosophically, the "African" in this ethics has the being of the African at stake. It is more than what a lawyer should or should not do ethically. Essentially, it is a matter of African anthropology – a matter of bringing into relief what it is to be an African.

Notes

1 G.W.F. Hegel, *The Philosophy of History*, trans. J. Sibree, intro. C.J. Friedrich. New York: Dover Publications, 1956.
2 Frantz Fanon, *The Wretched of the Earth*, trans. Richard Philcox. New York: Grove Press, 2004, p. xliii.
3 Giorgio Agamben, *What is Philosophy?* trans. Board of Trustees of the Leland Stanford Junior University. Stanford, CA: Stanford University Press, 2018, p. 1.
4 Frantz Fanon, *Black Skin, White Masks*, trans. Charles Lam Markmann. London: Pluto Press, 2008, p. 8.
5 Ibid., p. 9.

Chapter 3

African African jurisprudence in African African legal ethics

There is an African jurisprudence that is generated by non-Africans – a jurisprudence that is imposed on Africans. It is a jurisprudence that is exported to Africa, primarily by Europeans but also by Muslims. There is also an African jurisprudence that is indigenously generated by Africans. It is this jurisprudence that I refer to as African African jurisprudence. It is important to clarify what is African about African jurisprudence if this jurisprudence is to cast light on African African legal ethics – an ethics that is different from an African legal ethics exported to Africa by non-Africans. The clarification entails bringing to light the kind of conception and thinking that helps us explore and illuminate what is distinctive about African African jurisprudence.

The relation between African African jurisprudence and African African legal ethics is subject to multiple conceptions. I am neither a jurist nor a scholar, and the relevance of what they say to what I say on the topic at hand is apparently marginal. What I bring to this topic is a philosophical perspective – a perspective that is immanent in what is said about the topic and that guides what is said. Narrowing it further, I have in mind an African philosophical perspective – a perspective that is still in the making not because it is African but because it is the very nature of a philosophical perspective whether African or non-African to always be in the making. Moreover, this perspective is not to be construed as a phenomenon invented by the Greeks or by the Euro-West. A philosophical perspective is local. It germinates locally. Accordingly, as it applies to the topic at hand it is indigenously African. An authentic philosophical perspective that operates in what I said has African roots – hence the relevance of the qualification of African jurisprudence and African legal ethics as African.

Jurisprudence can be construed as the science of law or as philosophy of law. Either construction is bedeviled by multiple issues. When construed as science, it is not clear how science is to be understood in this context. In modern Euro-Western thinking, science falls into multiple categories. It is assumed that here is a province of the natural and biophysical science that is differentiated from the province of the social sciences. I know of no claim where it is asserted that, as a science, jurisprudence belongs to the natural or biophysical science. Even in the case of natural law, it is not clear what is to be taken as the natural biophysical sense of law. As a science, jurisprudence is normally placed in the domain of social science. Why it is referred to as science is yet to be fully worked out and placing it in a province shared by other social sciences does not clarify its scientificity. In addition, the difference between the two provinces of science is still to be worked out. Barring conventional wisdom, the boundary that separates them remains tenuous. The crisis of European sciences has already been noted by Edmund Husserl in his work the *Crisis of European Sciences and Transcendental Phenomenology*.[1] Even if jurisprudence is accorded scientific status, Euro-Western scientific discourse – the reigning discourse in the world today – has little room for ethics. In the context of this discourse, linking African African jurisprudence with African African legal ethics is problematic, unless, of course, ethics is granted scientific status. Without clarifying what constitutes scientific status the linkage will be equally problematic.

During the nineteenth and twentieth centuries, in the Euro-West, great effort was exerted to endow the social sciences with genuine scientific status, which entailed the emulation of natural/biophysical science by excluding ethics and morality. If the study of law was to acquire scientific status, it had to meet the criteria for being scientific. I believe it was part of the attempt to endow jurisprudence with scientific status that led John Austin (an English legal theorist) to embark on the effort to demarcate the province of jurisprudence. He claimed that

> [t]he science of Jurisprudence (or simply and briefly, jurisprudence) is concerned with positive laws, or with laws strictly so called, as considered without regard to their goodness or badness.[2]

He also claimed that

> [t]he existence of law is one thing; its merit or demerit is another. Whether it be or not be is one inquiry; whether it be

> or be not conformable to an assumed standard, is a different inquiry. A law, which actually exists, is a law, though we happen to dislike it, or though it may vary from the text, by which we regulate our approbation or disapprobation.[3]

In his eyes, if jurisprudence were to gain scientific status it had to dispense with ethics or with morality. Linking ethics with law could only render the concept of jurisprudence nonsensical. This view contributed to what came known as legal positivism. The basic legal positivist dogma was belief in the separation between law and morality. H.L.A. Hart wrote an informative essay on this separation.[4]

The belief held by Austin that law is law and nothing else is undermined by his claim that law is a command emanating from a political superior. If it emanates from a political superior, it should be evident that politics is the foundation of law, and jurisprudence is inconceivable without politics. What is determined by Austin as the province of jurisprudence is, ultimately, a province of politics. The legal is the political. Because the political is superior or supreme, the separation of the legal from the ethics or from morality is inevitably a political decision. Moreover, since the aim of politics is to attain what is deemed to be societal good, and since societal good is a central feature of ethics or a central feature of morality, ultimately, law is inseparable from ethics or from morality. In other words, the determination of the goodness or the badness of law is relevant to what law is. In line with Austin's thinking, it appears that the claim that law is law and nothing else is false or, at least, contradictory. Accordingly, in his own determination of the province of jurisprudence, he cannot preempt ethics or morality. He sets the boundaries of jurisprudence in a way that is inconsistent with his own criterion of what is to constitute the province of jurisprudence. He gives a false sense of jurisprudence – a sense that surreptitiously promotes a version of ethics or a version of morality without disclosing what this version of ethics is or what version of morality is presupposed. It appears that law is ethics or morality by other means.

If one accepts Austin's view on jurisprudence, the attempt to link African African jurisprudence with African African legal ethics appears inappropriate or misguided. It is an attempt to do what ought not to be done, and the product is nonsensical. But one need not accept what Austin determines as the province of jurisprudence. However widely accepted, it remains an opinion among other opinions on jurisprudence. It could also reasonably be pointed out that this view of jurisprudence legitimized the enslavement of Africans, European colonialism in Africa, apartheid in South Africa, the subjection of women, Nazism, and wherever other deprivation of human dignity prevailed. A cover of their dehumanizing lawmakers, judges, and those who enforced the rule of law could be legitimized under the claim that ethics and morality are irrelevant to this rule. Consequently, launching an ethical or moral challenge to what was done in the name of the rule of law was irrelevant and unwarranted. Legislators were not legislators of ethical or moral laws; those who interpreted the laws (judges) were not interpreters of ethical or moral laws. Those who were called upon to enforce the law were under duty to enforce law and not ethics or morality. In their capacity as law officers, they were not moral agents.

What should not be forgotten is that Austin's view of jurisprudence is nothing more than one political determination of the province of jurisprudence among other political determinations of the province of jurisprudence. It is culture-specific and subject to historical context. It is a product of the political culture of the period in which he existed. In this period his determination was not exhaustive. It is also period in which the Marxian dialectical jurisprudence also flourished. Marx introduced the critical sociology of law in which he called attention to the bourgeois conception of jurisprudence – a conception shared by Austin. Austin's view served well the interests of the rising bourgeois capitalist class. The view provided legitimacy for the European colonization of Africans and/or other non-European people.

Contrary to what it may appear, when Austin's view is applied to other periods or to other cultures it has an ideological aspect – both political and cultural. The impression Austin gives that jurisprudence is a science of law obscures the contestable claim that this science is truly scientific. This obscurity is a disservice to jurisprudence, for it conceals the truth about jurisprudence. It shielded jurisprudence from dialectical critical scrutiny. It ends up silencing African African jurisprudence since African African jurisprudence, unhesitatingly, embraces ethics as its internal feature. Jurisprudence, as is the case with ethics, is time and place sensitive. Their linkage is equally time and place sensitive. Being time and place sensitive entails taking historical, social, and cultural contexts as essential venues for understanding both jurisprudence and ethics.

They are also essential venues for the understanding of how each stands in relation to the other.

There is no logical necessity for delinking jurisprudence from ethics. It could be pointed out that A is A implying that it is exclusively so, and B is B exclusively so, and then to conclude that it would be logically nonsensical to claim that A is B, or that B is A. However, we need to remind ourselves that reasoning in logic is not reasoning in law. Judges, lawyers, or legislators are not logicians. Deductive reasoning is central to formal logic, but it is not the kind of reasoning that applies to jurisprudential reasoning. Violation of the laws of logic is not illegal. It must not be forgotten that the existence of law is not an end in itself. Human beings create law to meet societal good, and such good is the subject matter of ethics. To rob law of ethics is an offense against law. Law cannot be its own justification for it would be before it is. It would fail to account for itself. If it attempted to account for itself by itself, it would say nothing substantive about itself. To deprive African African jurisprudence of its core ethics in pursuit of law in itself is to deprive it of its oxygen. When chips are down, legal positivism in its classical Austinian formulation cannot fare any better. It undermines itself. The kind of clarity that one finds in logic, especially in basic logic, is inapplicable to jurisprudence. If this is granted, other possibilities for understanding jurisprudence present themselves. These other possibilities include diverse philosophical understandings of jurisprudence. Austin's view of understanding jurisprudence represents a version of philosophical understanding of jurisprudence, but it is not exhaustive of philosophical understanding. It arises at a specific period in the history of Euro-Western legal thinking. It leaves out the history of African legal thinking as it does the legal thinking in the histories of other human communities.

Regarding jurisprudence as subject matter of philosophy, what is construed as philosophy matters. The Euro-West has embraced a monolithic conception of philosophy, thereby concealing the multiplicity of the sense of philosophy. There was a time when the mention of African philosophy generated scorn or laughter. Although this may not be as explicitly as it was in the past, today, scorn and laughter have not fully vanished. African philosophy is making an imprint on the landscape of philosophy and demands recognition. When African African jurisprudence is taken up by philosophy, one should expect African philosophy to play a significant role in determining its province. One of the major contributions of African philosophers today is the problematization of what is to be understood as philosophy. Little attention has been paid to how philosophy is to be broadly understood. The prevailing understanding of philosophy in the Euro-West is that philosophy is essentially a Euro-Western phenomenon. Applying this understanding of philosophy, it appears that, when applied to law, philosophy law is essentially a Euro-Western philosophy of law. In making a case for authentically African African philosophy, African philosophers are pointing out the illicit or erroneous move in projecting a Euro-Western understanding of philosophy as if it were universal. This universalization has contributed to the colonization of African philosophy, or at least to rendering it parasitic to Euro-Western philosophy. In Africa, the correction of this illicit or erroneous move entails the decolonizing of philosophy and, consequently, to decolonizing African philosophical jurisprudence. African African philosophy has its native soil in Africa. It is not an import from the Euro-West or from anywhere else. It is not a product of Euro-Western missionaries of philosophical jurisprudence. As a philosophy of law, African African jurisprudence is native to Africa.

Although not distinguished as a philosopher, Carl Schmitt, a leading twentieth-century German legal scholar and a sympathizer of Nazism, makes an observation on jurisprudence that is worth noting, as one thinks about African African jurisprudence. He says,

> We are aware of jurisprudence as a specifically European phenomenon. It is neither just practical intelligence nor only a handcraft. It is deeply enmeshed in the adventure of western rationalism. It comes as spirit from a noble parentage. Its father is the reborn Roman law, its mother the Roman Church. Separation from the mother was finally completed after centuries of difficult dispute in the age of confessional civil war. The child held to the father, Roman law and left the mother's home. It sought a new house and found it in the state. The new home was princely, a palace of the Renaissance or the Baroque. Jurists felt proud and far superior to the theologians.[5]

In his eyes, jurisprudence has its essential home in Europe. If he is right, African jurisprudence can only be seen as a child of European jurisprudence. That is, in its own right, the concept of African African jurisprudence is empty of content. Apparently, a jurisprudence that is independent of European jurisprudence is without content. And without content, there would be nothing to link to African African ethics. Authentic African jurisprudence is not a part of the adventure of western rationalism. It is not a product of the clash between the Roman Church (the Christian Church and Reason). If the state is a product of this clash, such a state is not an African African state. It is a European state. Moreover, a jurisprudence based on such a state – the kind of jurisprudence Schmitt has in mind, is a European jurisprudence. It is not African. If there is to be an African African state, it is more likely to be a product of the clash between European colonialism and African indigeneity. Its attendant jurisprudence is anti-colonial. It must be a decolonizing jurisprudence. Moreover, since colonizing Africans deprives them of their human dignity, and because human dignity lies at the core of ethics, decolonization of colonial jurisprudence is an ethical process, whose objective is the recovery and affirmation of the African human dignity. Euro-Western historical trajectory is different from African African historical trajectory. The difference is manifest in the conception of jurisprudence.

African African jurisprudence does not have Roman law and the Roman church as its parents. Its parents are African, and these parents are not children of Euro-Western parents and have not been adopted by Euro-Western parents or by the offspring of these parents. This is the case despite the jurisprudential paternalism that the Euro-West has imposed on Africans via slavery, colonialism, apartheid, and neo-colonialism. Although it was not widely recognized, the African struggle for independence entailed the struggle for jurisprudential independence. The latter phase of the struggle was more than replacing Euro-Western judges and other officers or law or replacing Euro-Western professors of law with African professors of law. The objective was to firmly affirm indigenous African African jurisprudence – a jurisprudence in which indigenous African African ethics was an essential element in the constitution of jurisprudence.

The contention so far is that legal ethics is legal ethics in a jurisprudential context. It takes place and is intelligible in a jurisprudential context. An African African legal ethics is not an exception. It takes place and is intelligible in the context of African African jurisprudence. Accordingly, in making sense of African African legal ethics, it is proper that one pays attention to African African jurisprudence. In philosophy, and for a philosopher, jurisprudence is a matter of philosophy. It is philosophy of law. In African African jurisprudence, it is African African philosophy of law that is at stake. It is a branch of African philosophy. Any account of African African legal ethics that skirts around African African philosophy of law is bound to lead to an incomplete conception of African African legal ethics and, most likely, to an erroneous understanding of what it is.

African African jurisprudence: is there such a jurisprudence? Is it a "tribal" jurisprudence? An "ethnic" jurisprudence? A "racial" jurisprudence? An "ethno-jurisprudence"? Quotes are used in these questions to highlight what is already problematic about how the word "African" is to be associated with the word "jurisprudence," and how it is to be associated with the word "ethics." Moreover, raising these questions appears to single out African African jurisprudence. These questions are rarely if ever raised when speaking or writing about Euro-Western jurisprudence. For example, when speaking or writing about German, French, English, or American jurisprudence, the question about tribal, ethnic, or racial identities does not come up. This double standard applies to what is said or written about ethics. Whereas one is likely to hear or see the words tribe, ethnic, or race associated with Africans, one is unlikely to hear or see them associated with Euro-Westerners. This double standard preempts meaningful dialogue between Africans and Euro-Westerners and threatens intra-African dialogue if Africans embrace how they are defined by Euro-Westerners. It threatens how Africans understand how African jurisprudence stands in relation to African ethics. For Africans, African African jurisprudence and African African ethics, and how the two stand in relation to each other is a matter of African self-understanding – a matter of self-understanding without having this self-understanding mediated by others especially by Euro-Westerners. It is undeniable that today, there exists enormous pressure from the advocates of universalism or from the advocates of cosmopolitanism. This pressure, however, must be resisted because, for the most part, what passes as universalism or as cosmopolitanism is parochialism in disguise. Having suffered from racist colonial imperialism Africans should be particularly sensitive to this possibility. There is a need to decolonize universalism and a need to decolonize cosmopolitanism.

African African legal ethics brings together two areas: African African jurisprudence and African African ethics. How the two areas are related to each other is not clear. Hopefully, an understanding of African African jurisprudence and our understanding of African African ethics can contribute to our understanding of how law and ethics are linked to each other. The presupposition here is that our understanding of the African African concept of law can help us understand the concept of the African African concept of ethics and vice versa and, armed with such understanding, we can understand the relation they have with each other. Should this be the case, it would follow that the two areas are not juxtapositionally related. They are not external to each other and do not exist side by side with each other. How this is the case is not self-evident. A part of what binds them together is that both are African. Africa is the common bond they have with each other. But what Africa means in this context is not self-evident. Perhaps, how each is understood can help us understand what is meant by Africa. What Africa means is not to be taken for granted. It is more than one geo-physical territory among other geophysical territories. Both law and ethics can point out what is "more." Both can also contribute to the constitution of the meaning of Africa.

In modern history, a history that is largely a product of Euro-Western historiography, Africa is projected as a territory that is devoid of ethics. The objective of European missionary activity in Africa has been to fill the void with European views on ethics – views that are fundamentally shaped by Judeo-Christianity. The imposition of these views has transformed Africans into beggars of ethics. Africans have been subjected to European ethical paternalism. African ethical space has been colonized to the extent that anti-colonial ethics is largely reduced to anti-ethics or, at least, marginalized. There has been a systematic attempt to eviscerate, evacuate, and to destroy indigenous African ethics under the assumption that these activities were not a violation of ethics since there was no ethics that could be subject to violation. Under European colonial imperial rule, exposure to non-European versions of ethics has been proscribed for fear that familiarity with them may form a basis for challenging this rule. The ethics diet has been Euro-Western. Today, for example, Africans are exposed to utilitarian, deontological, virtue ethics, care ethics, and to other Euro-Western branches of ethics. Africans have been rendered parasitic to Eurocentric doctrines of ethics. For Africans, legal ethics has been mostly the application of these Euro-centered doctrines to law. These doctrines have not been neutral. Doctrines of ethics are more than doctrines of ethics – they have constitutive power. When applied to law, they constitute what law is. They are formative of what law is.

The imposition of Euro-Western legal ethics on Africans complements the imposition of Islamic legal ethics on Africans. In Africa, Muslims have contributed the erroneous belief that the indigenous African is devoid of legal ethics. For Muslims, there is only one and one true legal ethics, and this is the ethics found in the Quran and in the sayings and practices of the prophet and in the practices of the community of the believers. This view of ethics is formative of what law is in Islam just as Islamic law is formative of what ethics is. That is, legal ethics is Islamic legal ethics. The qualification of legal ethics with the word "Islam" is substantive. This word determines not only what law is but also what ethics is and, hence, determines what legal ethics is. Differently stated, Islamic jurisprudence determines Islamic ethics and Islamic ethics determines Islamic jurisprudence. This ethics is total as is the case with this jurisprudence. No true jurisprudence or true ethics lies outside Islam. No true legal ethics lies outside Islam. In this way of thinking it is senseless and sinful to make a case for an African African legal ethics that is divorced from Islamic legal ethics. One who seeks to make a case for an African African legal ethics – an ethics that is neither Islamic nor Euro-Western – finds oneself between a rock and a hard place. One finds oneself as a river in a very deep canyon, hemmed in by two very hard high rocky walls – walls that have a suffocating effect. Friedrich Nietzsche, a famous German philosopher once pointed out that "one should not go to church if one wants to breathe pure air."[6] The same could be said about a mosque: "One should not go to a mosque if one wants to breathe pure air." Millions of Africans believe as a matter of faith that their lives and destiny lie in the church or in the mosque. It is difficult to persuade or convince them they have mistaken carbon monoxide for oxygen. By faith, they believe that legal ethics arises either in from the church or from the mosque. What lies between the church and the mosques is the Devil's grazing yard – a yard where animism flourishes and where it is nourished by the Devil. The two hard high rocky walls are what the African African legal ethicist must fight against – an unviable task. The difficult and painful chipping of these two walls is implicated in what it is to think like an African African legal ethicist.

Legal ethics, as is the case with ethics in general, is a sociological concept. It bears on a human being as a social being. It is founded on this ontological status of being human. An individual human being cannot be ethical in isolation from other individuals. It is only as a member of society that he or she can be ethical. This membership is constitutive of what a human being is. Being human is unthinkable outside human society. But if this is the case, what is one to make of the notion of autonomy that is one of the pillars of modern Euro-Western ethics? Kant readily comes to mind and so does Kierkegaard. If society is so essential for being human, clearly it cannot be a product of a contract among individual human beings, or a relation between isolated individuals; otherwise, individuals would preexist themselves. They would be before they are which would be absurd. It is precisely this absurdity that colonial and racist imperialism that Euro-Westerners sought to impose on Africans and that they sought to indigenize in them. Resistance to the imposition and refusal to be indigenized in this sense led to the Euro-Western belief that Africans were savages and uncivilized. It may come across as preposterous that individuality to the African is fictional. Relationality exhausts what one is as a human being. One is one's relationship. A human is not to be thought of as an iron ball among fellow human beings who are similarly thought. The Euro-Western cult of individualism fits into this anthropological ontology and it is the ontology of that culture which Euro-Westerners have attempted to impose on and indigenize in Africans and on other non-Euro-Western peoples.

As a social being, a human being is not externally linked to other human beings. He or she has an internal link with them. His or her autonomy is not absolute. Contrary to the view held by Immanuel Kant, human society is not a kingdom of ends. Ends blend into each other in being what they are. This blending is not a matter of social contract as would be the case in the Hobbesian or Lockean sociology. Euro-Western social and political theory is the foundation of modern Euro-Western jurisprudence and also the Euro-Western theory of ethics. In both theories the primacy of the individual is paramount. In Africa, social and political theory, as is the case with the theory of law and the theory of ethics, the notion of *Ubuntu* is paramount. In this notion, a human being is what he or she is as member of the human community. In this notion, human individuality is not denied. It is recognized but it arises from communal existence. This communal existence is not an aggregate of individuals. It is the foundation of individuality. As John Mbiti once observed, "we are therefore I am."[7] The "we are" is not an aggregate of or a collectivity of individuals. It is an organic whole. This organic whole is the location of African ethics. An African African theory of law and an African African theory of ethics are rooted in this organic whole. *Ubuntu* is the foundation of both theories. It unifies both theories. It is the foundation of African African legal ethics and the foundation of African jurisprudence. *Ubuntu* is at the core of a jurisprudence that is truly African and a core of an ethics that is truly African.

In conventional Euro-Western legal ethics, legal ethics is what professors of law teach in their legal ethics courses. It is what law students learn in these courses. Law school is the primary location where legal ethics is taught. It is the classroom of legal ethics. Why can't society be the law school – the location where one learns legal ethics? Although this is not widely acknowledged in conventional Euro-Western teaching of legal ethics, Euro-Western society is the background of the legal ethics that is taught in law school. Geoffrey Hazard, a noted legal ethicist has observed that:

> In our society, most people who become lawyers have been brought up in a Judeo-Christian milieu and its corresponding morality. Their pre-law acculturation survives entry into the practice of law, so that most lawyers accept Judeo-Christianity as their "personal morality" and practice it in relationships with family and friends.[8]

The way that legal ethics is taught in Euro-Western law school conceals or takes for granted the underlying Judeo-Christian ethical values. When Euro-Western legal ethics is taught in the African law school these values are inevitably embodied in the legal ethics course. Law school becomes a conduit for Judeo-Christian values and a destroyer of indigenous values in African societies. Law professors become missionaries of Euro-Western Judeo-Christian ethical values. An important question to raise regarding African legal education is: What indigenous pre-law African ethics do African students bring with them when they enter law school – the ethics that after graduation inform their legal practice? One can imagine a Confucian ethics that undergirds the study and practice of law in Chinese society, a Buddhist ethics that undergirds the study and practice of law in a Buddhist society, Sharia ethics that undergirds the study and the practice of law in a Muslim society. It is not absurd to ask what ethics undergirds the study and the practice of law in an African society. Surely, the study and the practice of law in Africa cannot be an exception. It too must have an undergirding ethics. What is this central place in the study of philosophy. Even when a philosopher's specialty is in legal philosophy, it should not be forgotten such specialization takes place in philosophy and is ultimately accountable to it. That is, for these philosophers, the study of the nature of law is a part of philosophical study. Some philosophers inquire into the nature of law and those who do so are likely to make a significant contribution to an inquiry into legal ethics.

The introduction of philosophy into an inquiry of the nature of legal ethics is not extraneous to legal ethics. Legal ethics can be approached and, indeed, it is approached from multiple perspectives. For the sake of clarity, these perspectives should not be confused with each other. The audience is also diverse. There are those who approach legal ethics from the perspective of the legal profession. The audience in this case are members of the legal profession or those who aspire to be members of this profession. Generally, this perspective on legal ethics falls into the category of professional ethics for, although professions have their unique version of ethics, yet by being professions, they have common interest in professional ethics. In this case, the audience comprises those who have an interest in professional ethics.

African legal ethics may fall into the category of legal professional ethics or into the category of professional ethics. In the first case, the audience would be members of the African legal profession or those who aspire to acquire membership of it. In the second case, membership would comprise members of the professions or those who aspire to acquire membership in them. I choose a philosophical perspective to guide me in my approach to African African legal ethics. The audience is intended to comprise those who have an interest in philosophy or those who are curious about what philosophy can contribute to the understanding of legal ethics in general and African African legal ethics in particular. It may also be of interest to those who comprise the audience of the legal profession or the audience of professional ethics. Indeed, anyone who is interested in ethics may benefit from what philosophy says. Even more broadly, I believe that interest in ethics is a human interest and benefits all human beings. Philosophy can nourish this interest. Ultimately, it has the entire human community as its audience. In other words, even professional legal ethics and all other branches of professional ethics have the entire human community as their audience.

Although there are professors of philosophy, basically, philosophy is not a profession. If ethics is associated with it, it is an ethics that derives its raison d'être from the entire human community. One does not have to acquire membership in professorial philosophy or have an interest in becoming a professor of philosophy or an academic philosopher. Philosophy is embedded in all human beings. Accordingly, as a branch of philosophy, ethics is not restricted to professional or academic philosophers. When legal ethics is taken up in philosophy, any human being can benefit from what is said.

What is a philosophical approach to African African legal ethics is not self-evident. Partly, this is because what a philosophical approach is is unclear. If what a philosophical approach is is unclear, ultimately, it is because what philosophy itself is is unclear. If one knows what philosophy is, one will be in a better position to recognize a philosophical approach, and once there is this recognition, one is in a better position to understand how this approach bears on African African legal ethics. It is also important to recognize that African African philosophy is more likely to yield an approach that can contribute to a better understanding of African African legal ethics. Whether there is such philosophy was an issue for "African philosophers" in the second part of the twentieth century (I put this in quotation marks for, strictly speaking, if there is no African philosophy, there cannot be African philosophers). In part, the genesis of the issue regarding the existence of African philosophy can be traced to a deeply rooted view in the Euro-West that the association of philosophy with Africans is absurd. Africa, apparently, is devoid of philosophy, and what is found there has been introduced by Euro-Westerners. Also central to this view is that philosophy is not only Euro-Western but also it is the Euro-West that is the oasis and custodian of philosophy. Accordingly, anyone who seeks to be philosophical must turn to the Euro-West. The greed that has been a driving force in Euro-Western history has led to the appropriation of Greek and Roman philosophy by Euro-Westerners making this philosophy their own. It has been largely forgotten that neither the Greek nor the Roman philosophers were European philosophers.

In the light of the Euro-Western view of philosophy, a philosophical approach to African African legal ethics amounts to a Euro-Western philosophical approach to African legal ethics. That is, both law and ethics are determined as such by the Euro-Western philosophical cannon, thereby avoiding an Afrocentric view of philosophy and, consequently, Afrocentric legal philosophy and Afrocentric philosophical ethics. How philosophy bears on law, on ethics, and on legal ethics is substantially important. It determines law, ethics and legal ethics. It is precisely for this reason that Afrocentric philosophy matters. It determines law, ethics, and legal ethics Afrocentrically. Such determination cures Africans of dependence on Eurocentric philosophy or dependence on Eurocentric legal philosophy and of Eurocentric philosophical ethics. This is particularly important in this age of an international or global regime of development – a regime that has reduced Africans to the status of beggars and that has subjected them to foreign aid in philosophy. Being a philosopher is incompatible with being a beggar of philosophy. It is philosophically preposterous for Africans to view Euro-West as the sacred oasis for philosophical inspiration. For Africans, the sacred oasis for philosophical inspiration is in Africa. The Africa that is projected as without indigenous philosophical inspiration is not only foreign to Africans; it is anti-African. An African who stretches his or her arms with hands holding a calabash to have law and ethics placed there by Europeans is a disgrace to himself/herself and to fellow Africans. Whoever hands them to him or to her not only contributes to this disgrace but also disgraces himself or herself.

If Africa is not normally associated with philosophy, this is primarily due to a Euro-Western conception of philosophy. This lack of association is not simply accidental omission. It has to do with the prevailing Euro-Western understanding of philosophy. Martin Heidegger, a leading twentieth-century philosopher expresses commonly held views about philosophy in the Euro-West. He says, "The word *philosophia* tell us that philosophy is something which first of all determines the existence of the Greek world. Not only that – *philosophia* also determines the innermost basic feature of our Western European history," and adds: "The statement that philosophy is in its nature Greek says nothing more than that the West and Europe, and only these, are, in the innermost curse of their history, originally philosophical."[10] Herein lies the mortal danger of introducing a philosophical approach to the study of African African legal ethics. The indigenous African philosophical notion of African African ethics is rendered null and void, and whatever goes by this name is reduced to being parasitic to Euro-Western legal ethics. Once it is claimed that philosophy has no place in Africa there lacks an indigenous African philosophical foundation for African jurisprudence.

One cannot claim that philosophy is or is not associated with a territory without an understanding of the nature of philosophy. Euro-Westerners cannot claim to be the sole owners of philosophy without presupposing an understating of philosophy. This presupposition is erroneous and cannot truthfully guide us in the study of legal ethics or the study of ethics in general. If the word philosophy, in its Greek sense refers to the love of wisdom, one does not find among the Greek philosophers the nonsensical belief that love of wisdom (philosophy) originated in Greece or that the Greeks and only the Greeks were originally philosophical. It would be foolish to hold on to this belief. Greek philosophers were not idiots as they are made out to be by their self-made heirs. As a love of Wisdom, philosophy is to be found among all the peoples that make up the human community among whom are Africans. The view that Africa is normally not associated with philosophy is not an African African view and there is no evidence that it is a Greek view. It is a Euro-Western view – a view that has compromised the philosophical integrity of African legal ethics. African African legal ethics has indigenous philosophical roots in Africa among indigenous Africans. Under the regime of what the Euro-West understands as philosophy, what passes as legal ethics is law as defined by the 'barrel of a gun' and ethics as a legitimation of this law. In other words, legal ethics has been used to legitimize this use of force or the use of violence. The oppressors and exploiters of Africans have understood this to be the nature of law and the nature of its ethics. The administration of this force, this violence has provided legitimacy for what passes as legal ethics. African dictatorial regimes have learnt this lesson well. They resist the unmasking of what goes under the name of law or unmasking what undergirds the conception and deployment of law. Law was what was dictated by the oppressor's and by the exploiters. As the subjects of colonizing and dominating powers, Africans were duty bound to obey without questions. They were to do what was commanded; failure to obey meant jail, prison, or other forms of confinement or repression. In postcolonial Africa the question is whether legal ethics has ceased to be what it was during the colonial era. This question ought to have a prominent place in African law school. Currently, it does not for it is a threat to most African political regimes.

How philosophy and legal ethics stand in relation to each other cannot be fully understood outside politics. Amílcar Cabral calls our attention to an African proverb that says, "rice can be cooked only in a pot."[11] The pot in our discussion of African African legal ethic is politics. Both law and politics exit politically and so does philosophy. Thus, philosophy, law, and ethics have a common home where they are not strangers to each other. There is a common erroneous perception that philosophy is a thing in itself – a thing that excludes non-philosophy such as law; and similarly, there is an erroneous perception that law is in itself a thing that excludes non-law such as philosophy. One of the ways in which this exclusion is institutionalized is through education. Being educated in philosophy differs from being educated in law. A professor of philosophy is not a professor of law and a student of philosophy is not a student of law. Given these differences it would appear transgressive for a philosopher to speak authoritatively about legal ethics since legal ethics appears to be the province of a lawyer. A lawyer is projected as being more knowledgeable about ethical problems that arise in the practice of law than a philosopher. The fact that this state of affairs is thoroughly and deeply engrained is not beyond critical examination. The location of both philosophy and law can be contested especially if it is claimed that conventional topography of the education landscape is the only valid one. Law affects a philosopher not only because he or she can be a lawyer's client but also because like a philosopher, a lawyer is a human being. As a human being, a lawyer is not excluded from the domain of philosophy. Philosophy affects a lawyer and every other human being. Conventionally, it is assumed that law is a practical activity whereas philosophy is an impractical, speculative, or theoretical activity. The view that philosophy is not practical and that it is primarily speculative and theoretical impoverishes our understanding of philosophy. Properly understood, philosophy concerns itself with living well, and living well is a central feature of ethics. Ethics concerns itself with the principles of living well for the sake of living well. To this extent philosophy is a practical activity. If a lawyer is to fully distinguish himself or herself, he or she will inevitably run into a philosophy. That this does not appear to be necessarily the case points to the failure to understand both the scope of law and the scope of philosophy. It must be recalled that the lawyer's client is more than a client and expects him or her to treat him or her as being more than a client. The client deserves to be treated more than a client and so does the lawyer. Each ought to be recognized by the other as a human being. Broadly and adequately understood, this recognition is founded on the understanding of a human being as an ethical being. There is a need for the humanity of each to be recognized. Conventional legal education today is oblivious of this fact. The lawyer's professional ethics barely touches on this broader and deeper conception of legal ethics. What is human does not figure out prominently in the lawyer's legal ethics

I have no evidence to support the belief that the teaching of legal ethics in African law schools is different from the teaching of legal ethics in law school in the Euro-West. Other than a course on professional ethics, essentially, legal ethics is not taken seriously. Perhaps, this should not come as a surprise, for conventional wisdom is that one goes to law school to study law and not to study ethics. Resistance to the teaching of legal ethics in the United States law schools has been noted by Elizabeth D. Gee and James R. Elkins. In an article titled "Resistance to Legal ethics" they point to a not too unreal exchange between law professors:

> "What is the topic of your research?"
>
> "I am studying law school instruction in ethics."
>
> "But isn't legal ethics an oxymoron?"[12]

Such an exchange is unlikely to appear in African legal education not because the teaching of legal ethics is fully embraced but because, other than professional codes of conduct, it is totally ignored. Perhaps it is ignored because the teaching of law in Africa remains mostly under the regime of Euro-Western teaching of law. If in the Euro-West, legal ethics is not taken seriously, it is very likely it will not be taken seriously in Africa. Moreover, the assumption of what law is or what ethics is in the Euro-West is blindly transmitted in current legal education in Africa.

As the word "law" appears in the English language, for the most part, it is speakers of this language who are likely to understand what it means. There are millions, perhaps, billions of people who do not speak or understand this language among whom are millions of Africans. Failure to recognize the linguistic context of the meaning of law and its rule can lead to an erroneous belief that those who do not speak English share the meaning of the word law and its rule. The failure could lead to a false version of universalism. It is not to be assumed that what law and its rule mean in the West is identical to the meaning that Africans attach to law and its rule. Also, it should not be assumed that what the word "ethics" means in the Euro-West is the same as it means in African or in other non-Euro-Western territories. In the contemporary Euro-West, ethics is centered on an isolated individual, on an autonomous individual. In Africa, such an individual is an abstract or a fictional entity. In Africa, an individual is an individual in relation to other individuals. He or she is what he or she is through membership in a community – not a community as an aggregate of independent individuals by a living organic community (an *Ubuntu* community). This mode of being is not exclusive to Africans. There are other human communities where the individual is similarly situated. African jurisprudence and its attendant ethics emerge from such a community.

Evidently, as is the case with any other branch of legal ethics, reflection on African African legal ethics touches on law. It is beneficial to enter into a discussion on African African legal ethics via a discussion of the nature of law. This should not be taken as implying that ethics is subject to law for it could be the case that it is law that is subject to ethics. It could also be the case that each is subject to the other, which would imply that one cannot think about law without thinking about ethics, and one cannot think about ethics without thinking about law. Perhaps this kind of thinking is inevitable when one thinks about legal ethics, for the expression "legal ethics" implies both the concept of law and the concept of ethics. The relation between these two has been an important element in contemporary jurisprudence and should not be ignored. Fixation to branches of law encourages such ignorance. African African legal scholars are yet to be fully engaged in the discussion of this relation. One of the reasons for this state of affairs is that, for the most part, African jurisprudence has been subject to Euro-Wester jurisprudence, and even African ethics is heavily influenced by a Euro-Western view of ethics. This subjection was initiated when European colonial rule was instituted in Africa. Today, despite the independence of African nations, there have been no significant changes. In part, African African legal ethics challenge this subjection. The challenge draws inspiration from African African jurisprudence while at the same time it contributes to the construction of this jurisprudence. Thinking of this challenge in this way calls attention to its awkwardness: how can what inspires inspire before it is? This awkwardness cannot be set aside for it is intrinsic to this challenge. It is a challenge that is native to every essential thinking.

In Euro-Western jurisprudence, the word "law" is projected as if it has universal currency. When it is qualified as

Euro-Western the qualification does not render explicit the substantive aspect of this qualification. There is an assumption that the qualification is superfluous since jurisprudence is assumed to be jurisprudence everywhere. Law is law regardless of this qualification. Just as chemistry is chemistry regardless of its location jurisprudence, as a science, is jurisprudence regardless of its location. That is, the science of law is what it is regardless of its location. When Austin was determining the province of jurisprudence, the province so determined was not an English province. It was mean to be a global or a universal province whereby what law meant was the same everywhere. Since this position was not taken with Africans and with other non-European people, it became a source for the Euro-Western imperialist adventure in jurisprudence. This view of jurisprudence was to be imposed on all the people who make up the human community, and whoever resisted it was to be declared an enemy of law. African anti-colonial struggle and African anti-apartheid struggle were deemed to be contrary to law.

Law is law in the practice of law. Its jurisprudential nature is disclosed in in the practice of law. Ultimately, this is how law as law is known. To say that law is law as it is practiced is to call attention to the rule of law. How law rules in its rule there is disclosed what law is and how law is to be understood. If law is law regardless of its location, it would follow that the rule of law is the rule of law regardless of its location. Furthermore, by implication, the expression "rule of law" equally appears to have universal currency. When jurisprudence is qualified by the word "Euro-Western," this qualification is not simply a matter of geographical location or a veneer of law. It has substantive significance. It establishes a substantive definition of law and how law is to be understood. It is not to be assumed that the substantive definition of law in the Euro-West is the same as the substantive definition of law in Africa, and it is not to be assumed that how law is understood in Euro-West is the same as it is understood in Africa. Precisely for this reason it is an error to assume that what law is or what it means in the Euro-West has universal currency.

In trying to make sense of "law" it may be helpful to pay attention to the way that the word "God" is understood. The Hindus, the Romans, the Aztecs, the Mayas, the Africans, the Muslims, the Christians, do not have an identical understanding of God. The meaning of "God" is local but, as one learns in history there are those (Christians for example) who seek to impose their own sense of God on others. The sense of law is subject to the same understanding. It should not be assumed that it is the same everywhere. Mistaking what is local for the universal or imposing what is local everywhere should be avoided. What is true of the sense of "law" is equally true of the sense of the expression "rule of law." One of the major issues in jurisprudence is how to generate a dialogue between different provinces of jurisprudence, between different conceptions of law. In other words, how is a monologue to be avoided in discussing the nature of law? Clearly, this issue is a non-issue for the globalists or universalists who deny heterogeneity in the conception of law. Colonialism was cannibalistic towards heterogeneity of law. It autocratically declared that there was one and only one conception of law, one and only one conception of jurisprudence and that was the law and the jurisprudence of the colonizer. In Africa this view was reinforced by Islam. According to Muslims, there is only one true law and only one true jurisprudence – that is Allah's law and Allah's based jurisprudence *Shari'a* as it is revealed in the Koran. Either, under Euro-Western or Islamic jurisprudence there is no place for autochthonous African African jurisprudence; or there is no place for an African African conception of law. African African jurisprudence contests this denial, this voiding of African African jurisprudence not by instituting another jurisprudential monologue but pointing out the necessity of opening a jurisprudential space where a genuine conversation on jurisprudence can take place – a place where heterogeneity of the conversation on jurisprudential conversation is affirmed and practiced.

The inquiry into the nature of law rarely takes place in the context of the rule of law. An inquiry about this context is likely to make a significant contribution to our understanding of law. Whether explicit or implicit the rule of law entails a definition of law. I bring in Africa to bear the nature of law as it is exhibited in the rule of law to give an African flavor to it. There is no definition of law or definition of the rule of law that does not have a flavor. To not have a flavor is to be tasteless. What is tasteless might as well not exit, for flavor is not merely an outer coating of a phenomenon. It is what announces what a phenomenon is. It is how a phenomenon expresses itself as what it is. The rule of law is the flavor of law. It is what brings into relief what law is and what law means. What then, does the rule of law exhibit as the nature of law? As we seek an answer to this question, caution is in order, for there are multiple ways of looking at it. We should be mindful of the temptation of looking at it the way God would. This is particularly the case when one has a Christian God or a Muslim God in mind. Allegedly, God in either case looks at everything from all standpoints at the same time. We should be particularly mindful of those human beings who mistake their own standpoint for a divine standpoint. Among those who have fallen prey to this mistake is the German philosopher Hegel. It is he who claimed that:

> The peculiarly African character is difficult to comprehend, for the very reason that in reference to it, we must quite give up the principle which naturally accompanies all our ideas – the category of universality. In Negro life the characteristic point is the fact that consciousness has not yet attained to the realization of any substantial objective existence – as for example, God or law – in which the interest of man's volition is involved and in which he realizes his own being.[13]

Ultimately, for him there is an intrinsic connection between law and God. For him, law, fully understood is Divine. It is God's revelation of Himself to Himself as instantiated in the human mind – in consciousness when it is fully conscious of itself. To Hegel, Law is divine, and its rule is thereby divine. Knowledge of law leads to the knowledge of God and it follows that the knowledge of legal ethics leads to the knowledge of God. Because according to Hegel, there is only one true God, His rule of law is the only true rule of law. Just as God for Hegel is the universal being, His rule has universal validity. Besides it, there is no other valid rule of law. The God Hegel had in mind is the Judeo-Christian God who, according to Christian believers is the only true God. This God is not only the ultimate source of law; law's rule is His rule. True knowledge of the law and its attendant ethics leads to the knowledge of the Judeo-Christian God. In the above passage, the African referred to by Hegel as a "Negro," is yet to become conscious of law and its ethics. It would follow that if this is indeed the case, an African has no sense of the law's rule. He has no sense of the rule of law or a sense of legal ethics. In Hegel's eyes, Africa, it would seem, is a lawless continent, and Africans are lawless, and where there is lawlessness, there is no legal ethics. This conception of Africa opens the door for the missionaries of law and its rule. It opens the door to legal ethics missionary activity. In modern history, Europeans took full advantage of the alleged vacuum and sent missionaries of law to Africa to institutionalize the rule of law and attendant ethics.

To Africans, what Europeans took to be law is not secret. During the enslavement and the colonization phases of African history, law and its rule have meant the enslavement and the colonization of Africans. Law was what the colonial government said was law. It was the command of the colonial governor – the governor who distinguished himself by oppressing and exploiting Africans. The rule of law was the rule of oppressing and exploiting Africans. It was a rule of plundering Africa of its resources. It was the rule for governing Africans against their will. Back in Europe, law and its rule were different. Law's rule was the rule of self-governance. To Europeans, it meant government of Europeans by Europeans for Europeans. It was about the protection of European persons, their liberty, and their property. In the Hegelian sense, unlike Africans, Europeans had fully attained the level of consciousness of law and its rule. In their eyes, Europe was not a savage continent inhabited by lawless and savage people. Europe was civilized and was inhabited by civilized people. Europeans did not need non-Europeans or foreigners as missionaries of law and its rule to fill a void since such a void did not exist. Moreover, since Europeans had law and its rule, the concept of legal ethics would make sense. It would make sense to speak about European legal ethics. In European eyes, since Africans did not have law, there was nothing to which ethics could apply. In other words, it would have been nonsensical to speak of African African legal ethics since there was no law to which ethics could be applied. The concept of legal ethics was empty and meaningless. Africans could not send the missionaries of law and its rule to Europe or to anywhere else since they had no consciousness of law. Strictly speaking, law and its rule is not subject to missionary activity. When it is not conceived a missionary activity, it has an ideological message that violates human rights. Legal ethics in this context legitimizes this violation.

The perception of Africa and of Africans as lawless and as savages has another source: Islam. For Muslim law and its rule was revealed to Prophet Muhammed by Allah. It was embodied in the Quran – the holy book of the Muslims and in the sayings and the practices of the Prophet Muhammad. Law was the Shari'a. To be a Muslim, one had to be bound by Shari'a. Shari'a was binding because it was the Allah. Ultimately, law called for submission of oneself to Allah. Those who were not bound by it had no knowledge of law or the true knowledge of its rule. It is precisely this judgment under which Africans fell. From the early days of Islam in Africa, the followers of the Prophet Mohammed (Muslims) regarded Africans as infidels or as kaffirs – as a people who did not have true knowledge of God (Allah) from whom the knowledge of law and its rule could be derived. Africans were contemptable and not fully human since they were unbelievers. Under the assumption that Africans lacked the knowledge of the true God, Muslims saw Africans as ripe for missionary activity. Their objective was to convert Africans to Islam so that they could have true knowledge of law and its rule. Once they converted to Islam, there was a law to which ethics could attach. African legal ethics would be Muslim legal ethics once Africans converted to Islam. Apparently, apart from Islam, the African concept of legal ethics would be devoid of content since there was no law to which ethics could apply. As was the case with the concept of law that Euro-Westerners introduced in Africa, the concept of law introduced by Muslims in Africa was tyrannical and oppressive to Africans. The rule of law was a rule of dehumanizing Africans. In either case, legal ethics entailed deprivation of Africans of their human rights – the rights to be human.

Today, a large portion of Africa is under Shari'a and a large portion of the it is under the Euro-Western conception of law. Other than the prejudices of Islamic jurisprudence and the prejudices of Euro-Western jurisprudence, deeply rooted and broadly spread is silence on African jurisprudence. Of course, those who deny the existence of law in indigenous Africa will claim that indigenous African jurisprudence is silenced is nonsensical. Since indigenous Africa is viewed as lawless, there is no jurisprudence there to be silenced. Where there is no law, there is no jurisprudence. But whoever claims that there is no indigenous law in Africa must have a criterion of what law is. Non-Africans cannot assume that their criterion applies universally and that it applies to the African criterion of what constitutes law.

What Europeans and Muslims have done in Africa is to impose on Africans what constitutes law and its rule. It is this imposition that applied in Islamized Africa, in colonial Africa, and in apartheid Africa. Both Christianity and Islam have not only constituted law and its rule but they have also brought ethics into it. In both religions, God is presented as the source of ethics. Consequently, the concept of legal ethics is deeply rooted in religion. Moreover, since the followers of both religions claim that Africans are heathens and hence without true theology or true religion it is absurd to speak of genuine African legal ethics. Both religions reduce Africans to beggars of God and to beggars of religion. They reduce Africans to beggars of other people's Gods and beggars of other people's religions, and to the extent that law and its rule has a theological and a religious foundation, Africans are also reduced to being beggars of other people's law and its rule of law. And, of course Christians and Muslims are more than willing to oblige. Indeed, they take it to be their religions' duty to undertake a missionary activity to help African beggars. The followers of these religions are obligated to be compassionate. After all African beggars are their beggars. They create Africans as their beggars. Africans flock into churches and into mosques without recognizing the historic harm they are doing to themselves. They are unaware of the cost they have incurred from spiritual and religious imperialism – an imperialism that has grave implications for their human dignity and human well-being. In their struggle against slavery, colonialism, and apartheid, at their peril they leave out spiritual and religious colonization and spiritual and religious imperialism. They suffer from historic amnesia similar to the amnesia that Europeans suffer from non-Europeans. Europeans, it must not be forgotten are spiritual and religious beggars. Christianity is not native to Europe. It was brought to Europe from the Middle East initially by Christianized Romans. They were convinced or compelled to admit that they were devoid of true spirituality and of true religion. Once turned into spiritual and religions beggars, they accepted this beggarliness and then set out to spread this beggarliness to the rest of the world. They are still doing so today. They appear to be embarrassed about their indigenous religiosity and spirituality and seek to make others feel the same way. Today, the Euro-Western landscape is populated by spiritual and religious beggars. In their own home they are spiritually and religiously homeless. They look up to the Middle East – to Bethlehem and Jerusalem to spiritually and religiously nourish themselves. Having converted to Christianity they developed a concept of law and a concept of ethics to whitewash their homelessness. When Nietzsche attempted to awaken them to what was taking place, he came across to them as a madman. He presented himself to them as such to dramatize the depth of their ignorance. In the name of religion, in the name of law, and in the name of ethics, Euro-Westerners have been on a crusade to spread their ignorance and their sense of homelessness to

Africans and to other non-Westerners. In Africa, they seek nothing short of uprooting or dislocating Africans from Africa, rendering them homeless in their own homeland, and enticing them to adopt the belief that the Euro-West is their real and true homeland. Euro-Western legal ethics is one of the agents of bringing this about.

If jurisprudence and its attendant ethics are to have a theological or religious foundation, African jurisprudence and its attendant ethics cannot be truly African if is it founded on other people's theology or on other people's religion. It cannot be parasitic to Christian theology or Christian religion, and it cannot be parasitic to Islamic theology or Islamic religion. It must have its foundation on African theology and African religion. Making a case for such a theology or religion is an extremely difficult task. It requires a radical challenge to the monopoly of theology and monopoly of religions by Christians and Muslims. To be successful, the challenge must be launched not only by African theologians of African theology or by African theoreticians of religion but by all Africans. African theoreticians of African legal ethics have a major role to play in this challenge and their success depends on the collaboration of other African theoreticians. As stated earlier, Christians and Muslims have defined Africans as a people without the knowledge of true God or the knowledge of the true religion. The relation that Africans have with the Muslims and Christians is radically unlike the relationship they have with indigenous religious peoples of Asia or the religious people of the pre-Colombian America. Christians and Muslims have distinguished themselves as religious invaders of African. They have sought theological and religious conquest of African. Their notion of law and ethics are inimical to the existence of genuine African law and to the existence of genuine African ethics: To genuine African legal ethics. Followers of non-Christian and non-Muslim religions have not conducted religious crusades in Africa. Similarly, Africans have not conducted religious crusades either inside Africa or outsides Africa. Indigenous African religious are not proselytizing religions. They are devoid of missionary activity. To the extent that legal ethics is based on religion, one will not find in Africa missionaries of the rule of law or the missionaries of ethics. For Africans, law and ethics are native grown. Evangelism or proselytization has no place in African African jurisprudence or in African African legal ethics.

Euro-Western mass media projects Africa as a continent without the rule of law, as a continent struggling to institute the rule of law. When so projected, there are those in the Euro-West who find it had to resist a paternalist attitude towards Africans. They want to institutionalize the rule of law in Africa. They operate under the belief that without the rule of law good governance cannot be secure in Africa. What remains unthought critically is what is to be understood by law and by the law's rule (rule of law). Clearly, it cannot be denied that there has been discussion on the nature of law and hence its rule. One of the contemporary Euro-Western contributors to this discussion is Joseph Raz. He has claimed that:

> Rule of law is not to be confused with democracy justice, equality (before the law or otherwise), human rights of any kind or respect for persons or for the dignity of man. A non-democratic legal system based on the denial of human rights or extensive poverty or racial segregation, sexual inequalities and religious persecution may in principle conform to the requirements of the rule of law better than any of the legal systems of more enlightened Western democracies.[14]

To avoid the confusion, he insists that the rule of law must be nothing more than the rule of law. He informs us that, "if the rule of law is the rule of good law then to explain its nature is to propound a complete social philosophy."[15] He has not moved away from the legal positivistic position on law or its rule.

Every theory of the rule of law presupposes a social philosophy. Such presupposition is inescapable even by Raz. He fails to point out the social philosophy of law that is presupposed by his theory. Ultimately, Raz's conceals not only what a rule of law is but also what law is. Rule of law defines what law is and when it is inappropriately defined, law itself is inappropriately defined. As stated by Raz, the claim that "rule is law is rule of law" is devoid of substance. He does not tell us what rules in the rule of law and, to claim that what rules is law does not explain or define what this rule is. It amounts to saying that law is rule of law and the rule of law is law. He may be expressing a logical nicety which is essentially tautological and has no substantive content. But what he is subject to is not substanceless verbiage. It leaves the material dimension of the rule of law untouched. It silences an ethical critique of the rule of law and renders legal ethics inconsequential in the definition and in the practice of law. What he says is sweet music to other ears of the separationists – those who seek the separation of morality from law. Raz is not an isolated thinker on what is law and its rule. It is a major aspect of Euro-Western jurisprudence. It should not come as a surprise that in the Euro-West, law students and the bulk of their teachers would find it ridiculous to accept legal ethics as a central feature in legal education.

A rule of law is not an end in itself. It is not made by human beings for the hell of it, or because it is an interesting pastime. It is made to serve specific societal/political and cultural needs. When it is claimed that the rule of law is the rule of law and that, in it, law rules, what is concealed are these needs. But these needs cannot be concealed. Rule of law rules publicly, it is not hidden in the hearts or in the minds of human beings. This rule is preeminently public. The needs that it serves are not secret. They are exhibited by law as it rules. For example, the colonial rule of law was designed to meet the political, social, and cultural needs of the colonizers. In apartheid Africa, the rule of law was the rule that served the political and social cultural needs of the white minority. For Muslims, the rule of law was designed to meet the needs of Muslim society. In Americas and the Caribbean Islands, the rule of law serviced the needs of slave masters. Frédéric Bastiat, a nineteenth-century Frenchman states the obvious:

> In the West Indies, ever since the introduction of slavery, the master from fathers to sons have professed the Christian Religion. Many times a day they repeat these words "all men are brethren: to love your neighbors is to fulfill the whole law". And then continue to have slaves. Nothing appears to them to be more natural and legitimate.[16]

He also noted that:

> What more powerful means of rendering a people moral than religion? And what religion more favorable to peace than Christianity? Yet what have we witnessed for eighteen hundred years? During all these ages we have seen men fight not only in spite of their religion but in the name of religion itself.[17]

The knowledge of to what Bastiat is calling attention did not have to be derived from mystical sources. It does not require a theologian to bring it to the attention of lay people. It was the everyday reality experienced by Africans in Africa and in African diaspora.

What Africans experienced in the West Indies was experienced in the United States. Slave masters and their families were deeply Christian. Slavery was fully legally and ethically supported. Legal education and legal practice supported this dehumanization of Africans. A similar situation held true in Latin America. In Africa, Christianity fully supported colonialism and apartheid. Afrikanners were deeply religious and, in colonial Africa, the church oiled the wheels of colonialism. As Fanon points out in colonized Africa, the Christian church was the White man's church. It was a racist and an oppressive institution. The Christian Euro-West has been deeply supportive of the dehumanization and plunder of Africans. Islam, it must not be forgotten contributed to the dehumanization of Africans. By declaring non-Muslim Africans as infidels and treating them as such, they were in support of what Euro-Westerners were doing to Africans.

To get to the heart of the African African conception of law and its rule, it is important to set aside the non-African/anti-African prejudice about what law or its rule is. There is a need for Africans to liberate themselves from Euro-Western and Islamic conceptions of law and its rule. In this way, room is opened up to entertain meaningful speculation on what the law and its rule is in Africa proper. This is not an easy undertaking, for millions of Africans are under the regime of the European or Muslim conception of law and its rule. Colonial and neocolonial occupation and religious imperialism pose formidable obstacles to the reclamation of African law and its rule. To return to Africa proper for an African African conception of law and its rule, it is important to avoid the error or thinking of such an Africa as animist Africa. Animism is a pernicious concept construed by Euro-Westerners to distinguish themselves from the heathen, savage, and uncivilized horde. A better way of understanding this concept is to think of those to whom it is applied as animals. In other words, animism is animalism. Non-Christian and non-Muslim Africans are not animists: They are what they are: Africans. They do not have an animist jurisprudence. They do not have an animist ethics. If there is a need to think about them in terms of their religion, their religion is African religion. If religion is to be taken as the basis of jurisprudence, African African religion is the basis of their jurisprudence, and if ethics needs a religious basis, African religion is the basis of their ethics.

For many of us, what is understood as the rule of law is normally not at issue. We take it for granted that a rule of law is a rule of law. As demonstrated above, on closer attention, however, what is such a rule is not as self-evident as it appears. It is not my intention to come up with an uncontested clarification of what is a rule of law. Such intention would be unrealistic. What a rule of law is continues to be a contested issue and will most likely remain so in the foreseeable future. Furthermore, I will not attempt to catalog all the definitions of the rule of law if only because I do not know all of them and also because it is not my intention to undertake a survey of the definitions of the rule of law. My modest intention is to contribute to the ongoing conversation on the nature of law and its rule with special emphasis on its bearing on African legal ethics.

Law is law in its rule. The ruling of law discloses what law is. For those of us who were victims of slavery or victims of imperial colonialism, the rule of law was a rule of oppression, suppression, and repression. It was a rule of dehumanization. Evidently, this is not how the colonizers viewed law and its rule; otherwise, they would have viewed law and its rule as dehumanizing. The fact is that they did not. Today, what is troubling to some of us is that the prevailing conception of law and its rule, as it has emerged from the modern western liberal social theory, may conceal ongoing dehumanization. Let it not be forgotten that the rule of law as defined in the Euro-West has not necessarily been incompatible with dehumanization. Bastiat once noted that:

> When plunder has become the means of existence of a large group of men mutually linked by social ties, they soon contrive to pass a law that sanctions it and a moral code that glorifies it.[18]

One does not have to revert to the period of slavery or to the colonial period to recognize this view of law and its morality. As evidenced in postcolonial Africa, many African political leaders continue to replicate what happened in these periods. This time, it is Africans who are doing it to fellow Africans. As Frantz Fanon pointed out, "The ministers, private secretaries, ambassadors, and prefects are chosen from the leader's ethnic group, sometimes directly from his family"[19], and further notes that,

> the heads of government are the true traitors of Africa, for they sell their continent to the worst of enemies: stupidity. This tribalization of power results much as one would expect, in

> regionalist thinking and separatisms. Decentralizing trends surface and triumph, the nation disintegrates and is dismembered. The leader who once cried: "African unity!" and thought of his own little family awakes to find himself saddled with five tribes who also want their ambassadors and ministers; and as irresponsible, oblivious, and pathetic as ever, he cries "treason".[20]

In Africa, legal professional ethics, as well as what is taught in law schools as legal ethics, is largely a camouflage that conceals the ethical moral legitimization of the ruling elite – the elite that plunders their own nations. Law schools are complicit in this sordid affair. Law students are not taught what goes under the label of legal education or the legal practice. The politics embedded in legal education and in legal practice is reduced to neutral technocracy. It is deeply and pervasively veiled. One is indoctrinated into "thinking" like a lawyer and "acting" as a lawyer. The mystification of the rule of law that prevailed in colonial and apartheid periods is given a new lease in postcolonial Africa.

In the Euro-West, there has been an ongoing unmasking of the empyrean assumption about legal ethics and legal practice. In Marxist jurisprudence, for example, the rule of law that emerges from modern western liberalism is the rule of the ruling/capitalist class. It is primarily used to secure and promote the interests of this class and to inhibit and prevent the proletariat class from overthrowing it. It is a rule that justifies the exploitation and oppression of the proletariat. In feminist jurisprudence, the prevailing rule of law in the Euro-West is a patriarchal rule that keeps women under subjection to men. The Euro-Western version of law and its rule gave legitimacy to slavery and to imperial colonialism. It gave legitimacy to apartheid. It has given legitimacy to racism. It has given legitimacy to genocide in different parts of the world. None of this should be taken to imply that only the western version of law and its rule has resulted in the dehumanizing of human beings, for this would be false. Dehumanization in the name of law and its rule is an equal opportunity employer. No tradition of the rule of law is immunized from it. Many postcolonial African regimes provide ample evidence of dehumanization in the name of law and its rule.

It is indeed the case that the conventional understanding of the rule of law in the Euro-West has been projected as humanistic and its globalization is generally viewed as an agent of humanism. Euro-Western mass media is replete with the call of the rule of law from the Euro-West – the Euro-West that views itself as the custodian of the rule of law. What history has taught us, however, is that law or its rule has a Janus head. It may have a dehumanizing effect on one side, while on the other side it may have a humanizing effect. The difference between the two is not always self-evident. Those who embrace the dehumanizing side of law and its rule do not explicitly proclaim publicly the side they have embraced. They are often duplicitous. They project themselves as defenders and promoters of the humanistic rule of law and accuse those who call attention to this duplicity of undermining such a rule of law. Again, the classic example is illustrated by slaveholders who accused those who struggled against slavery of undermining the rule of law and, equally, those who struggled against imperial colonialism of undermining the rule of law. In Africa, opponents of apartheid were projected as enemies of the rule of law and so were those who participated in the liberation movements in various parts of Africa. After the formal end of colonialism, many African-headed dictatorial regimes did not abolish the law and its regime. Their deeds were carried out in the name of law and its regime. What one can easily be led to conclude is that what is law and its rule is in the eyes of the beholder. Given this possibility, it is unreasonable to commit oneself blindly to the rule of law, for one may end up committing oneself to what one ought not to commit oneself to. Blind fidelity to the nature of law and it rule could lead to the negation or erosion of humanism. As one of the holy books says, sometimes the evil one comes as an angel of light. It is unwise to place a definition of the nature of law's rule on a neutral zone where its effects are disregarded. Advocates of liberal jurisprudence appear to have succumbed to this un-wisdom by applying a veneer of neutralism on law and its rule.

It is especially important to be cautious about formal definitions of the rule of law. One should pay attention to the way that law actually rules if one wants to grasp what a rule of law is in reality. Of course, this does not mean that one should dispense with the attempt to formulate a theoretical definition of a rule of law. The point is that one should not confuse a definition of the rule of law with an actual rule of law. The latter may serve as a criterion of what one defines as the rule of law. Law is law as law rules. One does not have to be a dialectical materialist to see the point that Mao made when he said that "human knowledge can in no way be separated from practice" and that "practice alone is the criterion of the truth of man's knowledge of the external world."[21] We know what is law by paying attention to practice – to how it rules. A pragmatist view of truth could also help us make sense of what a rule of law is by paying attention to what in practice it actually means.[22] This is the way to make sense of law and its rule.

From the standpoint of the practice, a definition of a rule of law appears inescapably political. Even the attempt to flee from the political is itself political. The word politics must be understood contextually, in practice. The sense of the political has not been the same throughout history. Ancient Greece is the birthplace of this word, and lest we end up believing that the Greeks were the ancestors of the discourse on politics as is widely believed in the Euro-West and as Euro-Westerners would like everybody else to believe, it should be noted that even in the Euro-West, the word does not mean what it meant to the ancient Greeks. The word "polis" from which the word politics is derived is a Greek word. It does not have its origin in a European language. Ancient Greece was Ancient Greece. It was not Europe. It was Greek and not European notwithstanding the recent Europeanization of Greece. Ancient Greeks believed that human beings were political by nature. The Moderns (Europeans) believe otherwise. They hold the view that by nature, human beings are apolitical. They become political by choice. They enter contractual relations with one another and establish the political. For the ancients, a rule of law, in so far as it is political, is a rule of nature. The Moderns reject this view and claim that a rule of law is political because human beings make it so. If it is binding, it is binding because human beings agree to be bound by it. Although a rule of law is a political creature, the Moderns also want to put it above politics out of fear that were it to remain political it would degenerate into a clash of subjective interests which they believe is the proper domain of politics. In other words, law would be indistinguishable from politics.

The quarrel about the sense of politics between the Modern and the Ancients is an intra-western quarrel and should not be viewed or understood as a universal quarrel. Accordingly, when it is said that a rule of law is inescapably political the multiple senses of 'political' should be retained. If the word 'politics' is to be used in a pre-European indigenous African sense in connection with the rule of law, it has to have an African sense. In the African sense it must convey an indigenous sense of what it is to be a human being. In indigenous Africa, to be a human being is to be a communal being. In Central, Eastern, and Sothern Africa, this mode of being is referred to as

Ubuntu. This mode of being is not a result of a social contract. It pre-dates a social contract. Though not identical, it is closely related to the Greek word 'polis'. To the African, outside *Ubuntu*, law and its rule of law is unintelligible. Consequently, as one can imagine there exists potential misunderstanding between Euro-Westerners and Africans when it comes to the understanding of law and its rule. What appears incontrovertible is that Euro-Westerners have attempted to impose their sense of law and its rule on Africans in the crusade to bring modernity to Africans. Ultimately, the attempt is to transform Africans into westerners. Such transformation is a violation of human dignity. It is a violation of the right to be human. It is contrary to humanism – at least to the type of humanism that emerges in *Ubuntuism*.[23]

When linked to ethics, an abstract conception of law (jurisprudence) generates a legal ethics that is abstract. Similarly, when law is linked to an abstract conception of ethics, it generates a conception of legal ethics that is abstract. In each case, abstractness rules. A legal ethicist has a choice to make either to be a servant of this regime or to be a servant of an opposing regime – a regime that recognizes that legal ethics is concretely situated, and to be concretely situated is to be situated historically, socially, and culturally. For the African African ethicist, it is a matter of coming to terms with his or her historical, social, and cultural situation – a situation that is not historically, socially, and culturally frozen. An African African legal ethicist cannot dispense with these contexts. For it is only by being contextual that he or she can appropriate and be appropriated by African African legal ethics. An African African legal ethicist must choose what he or she chooses to serve. He or she cannot avoid making a legal-ethical choice: abstract or concrete legal ethics. The choice that one makes guides one's legal practice if one chooses to practice law. Equally, it must be understood that non-African legal ethicists do not function without making a choice. Decontextualized legal ethics is a fraud. It obscures the substance of legal ethics and its attendant jurisprudence.

Notes

1 See Edmund Husserl, *Crisis of European Sciences and Transcendental Phenomenology*, trans. David Carr. Evanston, IL; Northwestern University Press, 1970.
2 John Austin, *The Province of Jurisprudence Determined* Hackett Publishers, Inc., Indianapolis, IN: Hackett, 1998, p. 126.

3 Ibid., p. 184.
4 See H.L.A. Hart, "Separation of Law from Morals," *Harvard Law Review* 71(4): 594, 1957.
5 Carl Schmitt, *Ex Captivitate Salus*, trans. Mathew Hannah. Cambridge: Polity Press, 2017, p. 56.
6 Friedrich Nietzsche, *Beyond Good and Evil*, trans. Walt Kaufmann. New York: Random House (Vintage), 1966, p. 43.
7 John Mbiti, *African Religions and Philosophy*. Garden City, NY: Doubleday, 1970, p. 189.
8 Geoffrey Hazzard, "The Morality of Law Practice," *Hastings Law Journal* 66(359): 371, Feb. 2015.
9 Karl Marx and Friedrich Engels, *The Manifesto of the Communist Party*. London: Penguin Random House, 2014(1848).
10 Martin Heidegger, *What is Philosophy?* trans. Jean T. Wilde and William Kluback. Albany, NY: New College University Press, 1956.
11 Amílcar Cabral, *Unity and Struggle*, trans Michael Wolfers. New York: Monthly Review Press, 1979, p. 116.
12 Elizabeth D. Gee and James R. Elkins, "Resistance to Legal Ethics," *Journal of the Legal Profession* 12: 29, 1987.
13 G.W.F. Hegel, *The Philosophy of History*, trans. J. Sibree. New York: Dover Publications, 1956, p. 93.
14 Joseph Raz, *The Authority of Law: Essays on Law and Morality*. Oxford: Clarendon Press, 1979, p. 211.
15 Ibid.,
16 Frédéric Bastiat, *Economic Sophisms*, trans. Jane and Michel Willens. Carmel, IN: Liberty Fund, 2016, p. 114.
17 Ibid., p. 116.
18 Ibid., p. 114.
19 Frantz Fanon, *The Wretched of the Earth*, trans. Richard Philcox. New York: Grove Press, 2004, p. 126.
20 Ibid., 126.
21 See Mao Tsetung, *Five Essays on Philosophy*. Peking: Foreign Languages Press, 1977, p. 4.
22 See William James, Pragmatism. Indianapolis: Hackett, 1981, Lecture VI "Pragmatism's Conception of Truth."
23 Ubuntuism is a way of thinking that has gained traction in South Africa although it is not exclusively restricted to South Africa. It is an expression of the view that one is a human being in a community with other human beings. It is a world related to Ujamaa as understood by Julius Nyerere and by John Mbiti who are credited with coining the expression "We are therefore I am."

Chapter 4

African African legal ethics as an expression of African African culture

Not all African legal ethics is generated by Africans. A branch of it is generated by Africans and the other is generated by non-Africans. The chapter focuses attention on the former: an African African legal ethics. Likewise, there is an African culture generated by Africans, and there is an African culture generated by non-Africans. This chapter focuses attention on the former: African African culture. Today, it is difficult to identify the difference because of the intermingling that has taken place. Moreover, the intermingling is going to continue. The existence of intermingling, however, should not discourage one from working out the difference. What should be borne in mind is caution as one works out the difference. The relation between African African legal ethics and African African culture is an internal one. One is a key to the understanding of the other. The dynamics in one exemplifies the dynamics in the other. Each feeds and is fed by the other.

There is no legal theory that exists in a societal or cultural vacuum just as there is no ethical theory that exists in a societal or cultural vacuum. Social existence is the foundation of legal ethics. An individual living in isolation from other individuals is not subject to law or to ethics. Legal ethics would not apply to him or to her. It is applicable to an individual only as a social being. It should then be obvious that African legal ethics is to be understood as a feature of African social existence – existence that is inescapably historical. There is no social existence that is cast in stone. All social existence is both temporal and historical. It is also to be noted that there is no social existence in a cultural vacuum. Culture is the flesh of every social existence. African social existence is not an exception. Accordingly, African African legal ethics is necessarily embedded in African culture. African legal ethics is inaccessible if one does not take African culture into account. Every other legal ethics is embedded in its respective culture and cannot be fully understood if this embedment is not taken seriously.

In thinking through the notion of African legal ethics it should be noted that there is a qualitative difference between the expression "African legal ethics" and the expression "legal ethics in Africa.". Underlying the expression "legal Ethics in Africa" are several assumptions one of which is the belief that, strictly speaking, ethics is the same everywhere irrespective of society, culture, or historical context. As such, it could be said that legal ethics is a science, and hence it ought to meet the criteria for all genuine sciences. Moreover, if it is assumed that all sciences are subject to the standard of rationality then as a science, African legal ethics must be subject to rationality. According to conventional understanding, what is rational shares the same feature as science. It is so, regardless of society, culture, or historical context. To ensure that there is no deviation, "legal" and "ethics" in the expression "African legal ethics" must be subject to universal criteria of science and to universal criteria of rationality. That is, what is legal, as is the case with what is ethical, is so, regardless of the societal, cultural, or historical context. Hence, strictly speaking, the expression "legal ethics" has a universal meaning. It also appears to be the case that the qualification of legal ethics by the word "African" has no substantive effect on legal ethics. It is merely a geographical designation of the location of legal ethics. Let us refer to the people who hold this view as universalist legal ethicists. They are Hountondjianists as characterized previously. Those who hold a contrary view, we will refer to as contextual legal ethicists. They hold the view that legal ethics is contextual. It is subject to society, culture, and to the historical context in which it exists.

The universalist legal ethicists obfuscate what is claimed by contextual legal ethicists by imposing a contextual view that is disguised as universalist. In other words, the universalism of the legal ethicists is a false universalism. It pretends to be what it is not. In colonial and in neocolonial Africa an attempt is made for colonialists neocolonialists to institutionalize and perpetuate this falsehood. The colonizer's and neocolonialist's false universalism – contextual legal ethics – is projected as if it were universal legal ethics. For universalist legal ethicists, Africa was taken to be nothing more than a geographical location for apparently universal legal ethics. For contextual legal ethicists,

"Africa" in the expression "legal ethics in Africa" is more than a geographical location of legal ethics. It stands for African society, African culture, and African historical context. In other words African society, African culture, and African historical contexts condition the understanding of legal ethics. The "in" in the expression "legal ethics in Africa" gives the wrong impression that Africa is an empirical container of legal ethics making it appear erroneously as if African legal ethics is not a part of African society, or a part of African culture. African legal ethics is a key to the understanding of African society and African culture. It is itself a product of African society and African culture. African society and culture are keys to understanding it.

Law is not only a product of culture. It also produces culture. Accordingly, thinking about law in a cultural vacuum is thinking without content. Similarly, ethics is product of culture and it also produces culture. Legal ethics is an ethics that is deeply rooted in culture. It is the flesh of culture. African legal ethics is deeply rooted in African culture and it is the flesh of African culture. Cleary, a study of African culture will inevitably discover that African culture is multiple. Undeniably, there are multiple cultures in Africa and there are multiple senses of ethics and multiple senses of law in Africa. It is equally true that African cultures today are influenced by non-African cultures, implying that ethics and law are subject to this influence. What is African about them is metastable. Every culture is dynamic and is subject to change. These changes affect the perception of legal ethics. African African legal ethics of yesterday is not the African African legal ethics of today and the African African legal ethics of today is not the African African legal ethics of tomorrow.

The African societal and cultural context from which African legal ethics emerges and that is constituted and serviced by it is inescapably political. This is not a situation that applies only to African African legal ethics. Every legal ethics emerges from its respective societal and cultural context and is inescapably political. A study of legal ethics cannot dispense with the study of politics. What politics is, moreover, is determined and shaped by the society and culture in which it exists. In turn, it determines and shapes the society and culture in which it exists. The politics of law and the politics of ethics must be taken into consideration in any serious attempt to understand law, ethics, and legal ethics. However, it should not be forgotten that what is meant by political needs to be scanned carefully, for its sense is determined contextually. In Kiswahili speaking countries of Africa, the world for politics is *siasa*. What is implied by this word is that politics is like a wrestling match, or more appropriately, a boxing match between two or more adversaries. The objective of the match is to have a winner and a loser. Each of the wrestlers does his best to defeat the other. There is no attempt to reach an amicable or harmonious end where neither one is a winner nor a loser. It also refers to a form of diversionary speech that obscures the seriousness of an issue that is the subject of discussion. This is the sense of the political that appears to have been imported to Africa by the Euro-West. It is party politics, fostered by the Euro-West as a mark of true democracy. Normally, African communities discourage this kind of politics for it is disruptive of the community.

As understood in the Euro-West, politics has given rise to the modern version of the rule of law and its attendant legal ethics. The key to this ethics is adversarialism. This adversarism plays out both in legal education and in legal practice. Students are taught to be gladiators and are expected to take this mode of thinking and to make it a foundation in legal practice. Debating is central to this kind of education and the better debater one is the more meritorious is one as a lawyer. The classroom debating is ultimately taken to the courts and the court itself because it is the pinnacle of the debate. Again, the objective is to win for one's client. In the *Second Treatise of Government*, John Locke, one of the architects of modern political theory, asserts that the chief end of government is protection of property. He says, "The great and the chief end, therefore, of men's uniting into commonwealths and putting themselves under government is the preservation of their property."[1] A rule of law, in so far as it is governmental, is established primarily to protect property. Each government frames a rule of law that secures it and that furthers its interests. Locke's view is important not only for the understanding of modern political theory and its related notion of rule of law; it is also important for the understanding of Euro-Western modernity in general. Some of the major products of this modernity are slavery, colonialism, and imperialism. These products embody conceptions of property. Slaves were the property of slave masters. Colonies were properties of colonizing countries, and imperial territories and those who inhabited them were properties of the imperialist countries. The implication of Locke's view on the chief end of government is obvious in these instances. Government was instituted to protect slavery, colonialism, and imperialism. Government was implicated in reducing millions of human beings into property but in preserving them as property. Since the rule of law is inherently associated with government, it has become the major instrument in carrying out a government's objective. Indeed, it is accurate to think of western modernity as a period in human history in which propertization of human beings became a historic project. The fight to preserve slavery, colonialism, and imperialism has been a fight to preserve or to secure millions of human beings as property and the struggle against slavery and colonialism and imperialism has been a fight against the "propertization" of human beings and to restore the humanity of human beings. In these fights there have been views of the rule of law that are in opposition to each other.

Law as the chief means of protecting property is the mantra of Euro-Western modernity and it is a mantra that the Euro-West has attempted to globalize. The measure of the integrity of the rule of law is the extent to which it protects property. For those without property, law and its rule is generally irrelevant and is perceived as a means of keeping them property-less. Money religion is the religion par excellence of our time. It is indeed the God of our time. One cannot afford to be an atheist. Perhaps, Americans know that better than others. Perhaps it is why "in God we trust" is inscribed on their dollar. This accounts for the popularity of law and the economics brand of law jurisprudence. Jurisprudence has been deeply embedded in capitalism. Capitalism lies coiled in the heart of modern legal ethics like a worm. It is at the core of modern legal ethics. Pressing for an African African legal ethics outside this version of legal ethics is like climbing Mount Everest. It appears utopian, especially since African lawyers have become converts of capitalism. They offer their services to capitalist African regimes. The fact that some of these regimes are riddled with corruption is not an accident. It is a means of survival in a life where money is worshipped. It is globally trendy. In this condition, legal ethics is a ruse, but it is projected as if it is not. It should not come as a surprise that legal ethics is not taken seriously. For the most part, the classical Hobbesian state of nature prevails: every man for himself. Traditional African ethics of care (*Ubuntu* ethics) is for idiots or for those who seek to flee from reality. Legal ethics turns out to be emblematic of the survival of the fittest. Ethical nihilism is the order of the day.

Although Euro-Westerners have claimed that the rule of law is to be viewed as apolitical, in practice, it is inescapably political. What has passed or what passes as the rule of law ought to be demystified to be truly understood. It is the effort to avoid politics that has given rise to the modern view of the rule of law – a view that has been eloquently stated by Joseph Raz. In his book *Authority of Law*, Joseph Raz, a well-known British legal philosopher, says that, "The rule of law means literally what it says: the rule of the law. Taken in the broader sense, this means that people should obey the law and be ruled by it."[2] In other words, the rule of law is the rule of law without qualification. It does not entail any other rule. One ought not to look outside of it to understand what it is. It is self-contained.

The claim that a rule of law is a rule of law does not really tell us much. If I want to find out from you what a cow is, telling me that a cow is a cow, does not get rid of my ignorance regarding what a cow is. Obviously, a cow is a cow and it cannot be other than a cow; but if I do not know what a cow is, you are not telling me anything that makes sense when you tell me that a cow is a cow. Obviously, I do not expect you to tell me that a cow is not a cow. I might as well not ask you what it is. When I ask you what a cow is, I am asking out of ignorance and I need to know what substantively distinguishes a cow from what is not a cow. In the case of the rule of law, what I need to know is what makes a rule a rule of law so that I can distinguish it from other rules. For example, I want to know what it is so I can distinguish it from the rule of morality or from the rule of religion. If the rule of law is the rule of the law, I need to know what law is so that I can recognize its rule. To be sure, one can tell me that if I do not know what law is, I can get an answer by looking at its rule because that is where it defines itself as law. This, however, is not helpful if only because for me to look at the rule of law, I must have a pre-understanding of what law is to help me identify its rule when I see its rule; otherwise, I run the risk of mistaking it for what it is not. Before making the claim about the rule of law, Raz informs us that the rule of law "should not be confused with democracy, justice, equality (before the law or otherwise), human rights of or any other kind of respect for persons or for the dignity of man."[3] Here, Raz is repeating John Austin's classic view:

> The existence of law is one thing; its merit or demerit is another. Whether it be or not be is one inquiry. Whether it be or not be conformable to an assumed standard, is a different inquiry. A law, which actually exists, is a law, though we happen to

> dislike it, or though it vary from the text, by which we regulate our approbation and disapprobation.[4]

In other words, law is law regardless of how it may be qualified. It may be unjust law, but it is still law just as a cow is a cow whether it is a sick cow or a mad cow. Qualifications of law do not affect its essence. In the light of this claim, one can also claim that "the existence of the rule of law is one thing; its merit or demerit is another." The rule of law is nothing more than the rule of law. It is what it is regardless of the qualifications that may be attached to it. Contrary to what appears to be the case, this view of law and its rule is *societal* and *culture* specific. Neither Austin nor Raz thinks in a societal or cultural vacuum. They are expressing social and cultural sentiments of their time. They are thinking in terms of the Euro-Western social and cultural existence of their time. Their time is not African time – it is their time.

The view of the rule of law held by Raz and its implied view of law forms a solid basis for conventional understanding of legal education. In law schools, law professors are expected to teach nothing more than law and law students are expected to and will learn nothing more than law. If there is an exposure to the rule of law, it will be an exposure to the rule of law and not to any other type of rule. Law teachers and law students are not to be distracted by the consideration of either the merit or demerit of the law or the merit or demerit of the rule of law. When students finish their legal education and enter legal practice, they will be practicing law and not something else. Those who end up becoming judges will judge from the standpoint of law itself and not from the standpoint of anything else. Those who are called upon to enforce the law or the rule of law will be enforcing nothing more than the law or the rule of law. Those who administer the rule of law will be doing nothing more that administering the rule of law. When called up to obey the law, citizens, equally, will be bound to obey the law itself and not question its merit or its demerit. In short, the rule of law will categorically rule in the light of what it is. If they dare ask why they should obey the law, they should be informed categorically that they are to obey the law because it is the law and it is as such that it must be obeyed. Everyone is subject to the law and to its rule. It is precisely this kind of thinking that allows for the marginalization of ethics in legal education and in legal practice. It provides a clear conscience for those who serve oppressive and dictatorial regimes – the kind of regimes that prevailed in colonial and apartheid Africa and in some postcolonial African regimes. In summary, though projected as socially and culturally neutral what prevails in legal education today is a legal education that is deeply steeped in a sociocultural situation that is primarily Euro-Western.

The view that the rule of law is the rule of law regardless of its merits or demerits, that is, regardless of the qualifications that may be attached to it, has a prominent place in the academy as noted. It has given rise to an autonomous zone where the study of law or the teaching of law takes place. Schools of law and faculties of law have been established specifically to study law. A substantive autonomous subject area in the academy is attractive to law teachers who, like their fellow colleagues, look for a separate area where they can distinguish themselves by what they teach. Law professors or law students should not be deprived of an area where they can distinguish themselves as such. It would be unfair to them since other citizens of the academy have their designated areas of teaching or areas of study. But it should also be borne in mind that the autonomy of academic disciplines is not sacrosanct. The current topography of the academy does not have to be the way it is. It may have outlived its time. If the Moderns have rejected antiquity, it is possible that modernity itself will be rejected. Rejectionism is a necessary feature of history.

Other than the consideration of professionalism and the disciplinary topography in the academic regime, there are other possible considerations as to why a rule of law is placed above politics. One is the cult of objectivism – a cult that has been fueled by modern science. Modern science, at least in its classical sense, demands objectivism. It demands the subject matter that one studies be independent of oneself and that he or he who studies does not inject his or her subjective views into what he or she studies. Those who seek truth about any phenomenon should set aside their subjective prejudices and let the phenomenon they are studying speak for itself or disclose itself in the very way that it is. In this study's conceptual framework, the study of law or the study of its rule should be scientific. It should be objective. Law is law and is out there independently of us. The rule of law is the rule of law and is out there independently of us. Independence of the judiciary is demanded by the very nature of law and its rule and not by the judges or by the lawmakers. Judges interpret the law; they do not make it. They are bound by it. It is already there existing independently of them and they judge according to its dictates. They are subject to law and its rule. If law is to retain its integrity as a law and if it is to rule, judges should obey it in their deliberations and judgments. Strictly speaking, they should be in the business of interpreting law and not in the business of making it. Likewise, where there is a jury, the jury is to make its decision based on law that is already in place and not introduce into their decision subjective considerations. The police and other law enforcement agencies are to enforce the law that is already there and not the one they make. Neutrality, non-partisanship, and impartiality become essential considerations on law and its rule.

Objectivism – the spirit of externalism that modernity has brought into prominence – is traceable not only to scientism but also to what has shaped it. Scientism is not irreducible. Descartes, the acknowledged father of modern western European philosophy has made a significant contribution to it. He does this by prioritizing independence, the certainty and existence of the mind (the thinking thing) over matter. Mind is projected as what it contrasts with the material world whose existence if demonstrable is independent of mind. He also finds in his mind the idea of God whose existence is necessary for his own existence and for the existence of the external world. His theology is Judeo-Christian. His God is a Judeo-Christian God – the God who has become domesticated in the western European world. He is a god who is transcendent and supernatural. Out of this theology there arises a jurisprudence, in which God (a being independent of us) is the ultimate source of Law, the ultimate Legislator, the ultimate Chief Justice, and the ultimate Executor of the Law. This is also a view that is central in Islamic jurisprudence. Despite the rise of secularism this belief remains at the core of law and its rule as understood not only in the western European world but also at the core of Islamic jurisprudence. Carl Schmitt has correctly pointed out:

> All significant concepts of the modern theory of the state are secularized theological concepts not only because of their historical development – in which they were transferred from theology to the theory of the state, whereby for example, the omnipotent God became the omnipotent lawgiver – but also because of their systematic structure, the recognition of which is necessary for a sociological consideration of these concepts. The exception in jurisprudence is

> analogous to the miracle in theology. Only by being aware of this analogy can we appreciate the manner in which the philosophical ideas of the state developed in the last centuries.[5]

Because of the close connection between law and state in the modern world, what he says about the state applies *mutatis mutandis* to modern Euro-Western jurisprudence. In short, what I am claiming here is that the belief that law is law and nothing else and that the rule of law is nothing more than rule by the law are beliefs that are essentially theological. They are expressions of a particular theology – the Judeo-Christian-Islamic theology. Legal philosophers in the Euro-West are largely theologians in disguise as are Islamic legal philosophers. To understand them as such the prevailing conception of law and the prevailing conception of the rule of law stand in need of demystification. There is a need to unmask the prevailing language of jurisprudence which will not be an easy undertaking because the mask has been naturalized to the point where for the most part it has ceased to be a mask. Let it also be noted that what has been masked is not simply the language of jurisprudence. Law and its rule are, ultimately, about being human or about human being. Every legal theory is a theory about being human. It is anthropology. Generally, this is not the view that law professors convey to their students and it is not what students expect to learn in a law school. Legal education is about law and its rule or its rules. Law professors are not in law school to teach anthropology but to teach law. Law students are in law school to study law and not anthropology. The study of anthropology is not a prerequisite for those who want to study law. In law school rulism rules, reigns. Central to rulism is the belief that the rule of law is neutral and impartial. Fidelity to this view of the rule of law is what law professors must inculcate in the minds of law students, and whether explicitly or implicitly it is conveyed to them that this is what it takes to think like a lawyer. In law school, students are neutered. They are rendered deaf to moral, ethical, social, political, and cultural concerns since these concerns would distract them from focusing attention on the study of law. The successful ones are those who demonstrate that, for the most part, they have met the demands of the study of law and its rule. Demonstration of success in law school is likely to serve them well when they enter the world of legal practice. Under this view of law and its rule, the globalization of the rule of law is the globalization of this way of thinking. What is globalized as the rule of law obfuscates multiple senses of law and, hence, multiple senses of its rule. It propagates a one-dimensional view of law and its rule and has led and leads to horrendous results in the human community.

What is conventionally said about law and its rule may not be what law is or what its rule is. What is said calls for a demystification. It must be unmasked. This will pay handsome epistemological and ontological dividends. Genuine knowledge of what law and its rule truly are will be made manifest. Legal positivism reminds me of a quote on what it is to think like a lawyer. Kelsen attempts to make a similar case for law itself. He legitimizes the existence of legal philosophers – philosophers who have fidelity to the law and its rule; but unfortunately this fidelity is self-undermining since they are trying to do the undoable. They are attempting to flee what they cannot flee from. The contradiction in which a legal mind is embedded is veiled by a rhetoric that is dominant in most of the legal education. One of the popular diets in law school is thinking like a lawyer. For those whose objective is to become legal practitioners, they clearly covet mastering the kind of thinking that will help them gain admission to the legal profession and that will provide them a prime opportunity for success in legal practice. As they are trained to think like lawyers, at the same time, they are rendered blind to the contradiction they are internalizing.

What legal positivists say is commendable as an effort to attain epistemic and ontological formal clarity in matters that pertain to law and its rule. After all, a thing is what it is by not being what it is not. When a thing is distinguished from other things, it can clearly be known as what it is and, clearly, not be confused with what it is not. This may make hypothetical epistemological and ontological sense but remains as such if one does not make any substantive claims. On the substantive level the distinction between phenomena may be more blurred in defiance of a formal/logical claim.

The way law and its rule is understood in legal positivism has, at most, a marginal place for ethics. The very notion of legal ethics is problematic in that it links law and ethics thereby compromising the purity of law and its rule. It amounts to an introduction of an alien element in the law and its rule. Hart has claimed that linking law with morality compromises the integrity of both.[6] The complaint that law and its rule may be dehumanizing is absurd since, strictly speaking, dehumanization has nothing to do with law and its rule. Law is law whether it dehumanizes or does not dehumanize. A rule of law is a rule of law regardless of whether it dehumanizes or does not dehumanize. Evidently, absurdity arises because of the way a law and its rule of law are understood. But law and its rule do not have to be understood a positivistic sense. Taking a non-positivist sense or even anti-positivist sense does not compel one to be an ethical relativist. What it forces us to do is to rethink what law is, and, consequently, what its rule is.

So far, we have referred to law and its rule from the standpoint of Euro-Western jurisprudence. This is not the only standpoint. The point is not simply to pay attention to other standpoints. It is, as said above to rethink what is to be understood as law and its rule. Perhaps there is more to law than law and more to its rule that bears on law and its rule. We can avail ourselves of this possibility by reflecting on the impact of Euro-Western jurisprudence on African social and cultural existence. As previously indicated in Chapter 3, Hegel claims that consciousness of law is yet to take place in the African. In his view in the landscape of law, the African is nowhere to be found. His conception of this landscape depends on his conception of law. We see in him a formulation of law that goes beyond conventional understanding of "rulism" of law. He has an understanding of law and its rule that takes being human into consideration. For him, law and its rule call attention to what is beyond law and its rule. What law and its rule call forth is being human. Law and its rule are ultimately about being human. For him, consciousness or the knowledge of law provides evidence for consciousness and knowledge of oneself as a human being. In law, one realizes oneself as a human being and knows oneself as such. The African lacks consciousness of law, and hence consciousness of himself as a human being. Moreover, if one lacks consciousness of law and hence consciousness of being human, it is senseless to treat him or her as a human being. It is irrational to treat him or her as if he or she were a human being. It is not contrary to law or to the rule of law to treat one who is not human as a non-human. The non-human deserves to be treated in a non-human way, since this is in accordance with what he or she is. Moreover, since law is law and its rule is its rule, morality has no bearing here. But even if it were assumed that morality has a place here in so far as it bears on being human, the charge that treating a non-human being as a non-human being is not immoral since it is only a human being who can be treated ether immorally or morally. Introducing morality in the domain of law subverts its integrity as law.

In the case of Hegel and those who think like him, it may be observed that one who misunderstands himself or herself runs the risk of misunderstanding others. Hegel had a cognitive and emotional disability that affected his understanding of himself. Had he paid attention to what the African had to say about himself, he may have had a partial cure for this disability. The fact is that the African that he talks about is a figment of his imagination, and the defect that he finds in the African are defects in the African that he imagines. It is not the real African – the Africans' African. Because of the defect attributed to the African by Hegel, the African is not self-consciously subject to the rule of law. He has no consciousness of law because his consciousness of himself has not evolved to the level where such consciousness would be possible.

Hegel's disability was both personal and more than personal. It was widely shared by fellow Europeans. Generally, it runs through European modernity. To a large extent, it is and has remained a part of European legal identity. One cannot fully understand the dominant view of law or the view of the rule of law without taking this into account. Modern European view of law and its rule provided legitimacy to the enslavement of Africans, to colonizing Africans, to subjecting Africans to apartheid, and generally to dehumanizing them. The dehumanization was extended to other non-Europeans but in the African it is more deeply rooted. For example, although Europeans regarded the native Americans as savages and lawless, they were deemed to be "Noble Savages;" there was nothing noble about Africans. There were savages in South East Asia and some generally in Asia, but Africans bore the brunt of savagery and lawlessness. Clearly, the modern western European view of law and its rule has provided a foundation and justification for planetary racism and planetary genocide. Planetary white supremacy would not have succeeded as it has without its support. The creed that white is human and that the human is white, and that the non-white is not human would not have been as deeply rooted in the human community as it is today without the blessing and support of a Euro-Western view of law and it rule. The creed has been the oxygen of white supremacy. It keeps white supremacy alive. There is no dancing around this. The modern European view of law and its rule is essentially racist. The view that law is law and the rule of law is the rule of the law and nothing else obscures this state of affairs. Blindness to this state of affairs has been institutionalized, naturalized.

Law is not an end itself and neither is its rule. Neither exists for its own sake. It is what it is, and its rule is what it is as a means to an end. The end is the human good. It is this to which law and its rule are subject. This end is specific to the individual but because the individual does not exist in isolation from other individuals, his or her version of what is good affects other individuals. It is an individual good as well as a social good. It is the latter because no individual exists in isolation from other individuals. It is indeed the case, as said on occasion, that an individual with regard to the collective good is a law unto himself or herself. One may make a law or a rule to govern oneself. However, the conventional understanding of law or understanding of the rule of law is that law and its rule pertain to individuals as social beings. No human being exists in isolation from other human beings. It is by existing with other human beings that one is a human being.

What one pursues as one's individual good must incorporate the social good. The good that is pursued by law and its rule is intrinsically social. What this implies however, is subject to controversy. The dominant view in the modern Euro-Western world is that society is nothing more than an aggregate of individuals and societal good is nothing more than an aggregate of individual goods. This view was formalized by the architects of modern social and political thought that include Thomas Hobbes, who many think of as its father. Moreover, according to this view, the social good is not natural. It is a product of social contract that individuals enter to remove themselves from the state of nature – a state that is characterized by lawlessness. Social contract brings into existence law and its rule. Neither law nor its rule is natural. Each is an artificial construct. What is important to note here is that the domestication of this view in the Euro-Western world has taken on an imperial form. Whenever and wherever Euro-Westerners do not see other people embracing this view, they assume that these people are living in a state of nature and stand in need of Euro-Western missionaries of law and its rule. They create a need for these missionaries in them and when they do not recognize this need or when they resist its creation, they are deemed to be ignorant of their own good. Those who remain non-human as Africans must in the eyes of Hegel have the need imposed on them since they have no clue what law or its rule is. They do not know their own good and they need Euro-Western paternalism to tell them what this good is. Under this imposition they experience law and its rule as a violent phenomenon. This is how law and its rule was experienced during the enslavement of Africans, during the colonization of Africans, and during apartheid. Being anti-slavery, anti-colonial, or anti-apartheid was illegal and undermined the rule of law. Moreover, in the eyes of Euro-Western missionaries of law and its rule, societies in which bonds among individuals were deemed natural were viewed as atavistic. These societies were to be destroyed by any means necessary to make room for modern societies where human good would flourish, where law and its rule would triumph. Law and its rule were used to bring about this destruction. The destruction was not presented as destruction. It was presented as a civilizing mission as a way of overcoming the darkness that prevailed over these societies. Africans bore, and still bear the brunt of this mission.

If it is granted that law and its rule is an instrumental good, this good defines what it is. No complete examination of law or its rule is complete without examining the good that it serves. Such examination is preeminently ethical. Why is this good ethical? What humanizes human beings? What is not good is what dehumanizes another human being. What does not lead to the exploitation oppression and repression of another human being? What does not rob another human being of his or her dignity as a human being?

Let it be recognized that legal rule or the rule of law has an instrumental sense. It is a means of attaining what law and its rule seeks to attain. It is not just a general social order. It is a specific social order that embodies the values of its members. This end is not a rule or a body of rules. It is the human good and it is this good that underlies the discussion of law and its rule. However, this is a conventional understanding of jurisprudence. What then is this good? The answer to this question is contextual. If the rule of law is taken as Euro-Western, its objective is the attainment and the securing of the good of the community – community understood as an aggregate of individuals. Individual good is paramount here. Accordingly, when we speak about the good of the community what is meant is the good of the individuals who make up the community. There is no organic community. In an African African notion of law and its rule, the good of this organic community is paramount. This community moreover is not to be construed in a way that dispenses with the individual good. What is to be noted is that the individual cannot pursue his or her own good at the expense of the other members of his or her community. Pursuing such a good is contrary to the individual's own good. Euro-Western modernity has institutionalized and is institutionalizing the undermining of this good. For the most part, this is what is meant by introducing modernity into Africa. Law and its rule, as understood in Euro-Western modernity, is the agent of this introduction and calls for a legal ethics that legitimizes this introduction.

It is ironic that in the Euro-West, there is an aversion to the affirmation of an essential link between law and ethics or law and morality while at the same time law and its rule are viewed as essential means of attaining individual good. For legal positivism (an important branch of jurisprudence in the Euro-West), the linkage compromises the integrity of law and its rule. Law is about law and about the law's rule, period. What is humanistic arises as a moral consideration and morality should not have a place in legal science. It has no proper place in law and its rule. Law professors are expected to teach law and not morality and law students go to law school to study law and not morality. A law court is a law court and not a court of morality. This is the lawyer-like thinking that the Euro-West has introduced in Africa. African leaders who are prone to authoritarianism feel threatened by the call for the introduction of ethics into law and its rule and find this to be music to their ears. Those who are engaged in legal education and in legal practice likewise find this cast of law and its rule to their liking. It does not disrupt what the are thinking or what they do.

One may look at law and its rule in two ways: from the standpoint of those who oppress others and from the standpoint of those who are oppressed: from the standpoint of those who seek to dehumanizer others and from the standpoint of those who resist dehumanization. The mantra that law is law and that its merits or demerits do not enter the definition of law make this distinction meaningless. But this meaninglessness is more than semantic squabbling. It can be a matter of life or death. Law and its rule matter in life. To say that they matter is to recognize the centrality of ethics in the conception of law and its rule. Recognition of the centrality of ethics calls attention to the dignity of being human or to what increasingly has come to be associated with human rights. To dehumanize others is to dehumanize oneself. In calling for the centrality of ethics in the conception of law and its rule, the dehumanized seek to affirm their dignity or their worth as human beings while at the same they seek to affirm the dignity of all human beings. Human dignity is indivisible. An individual cannot truly affirm his or her dignity at the expense of the worth and dignity of any other individual, and a group of individuals cannot affirm its worth and dignity at the expense of the worth and dignity of any other group. As Martin Luther King Jr. said:

> We are caught in an inescapable network of mutuality, tied to a single garment of destiny. Whatever affects one directly affects all indirectly.[7]

King was making his point regarding his fellow Americans during the struggles of the American civil rights movement but what he says has a bearing on all human beings wherever and whoever they are. He was challenging the segregationist law and its rule. Racism had torn the unity of Americans and King was speaking about healing it. He stood for what I am referring to as the humanistic rule of law. Close to his death he had come to recognize that racism was a planetary phenomenon and civil rights were essentially human rights. The kind of humanism he had come to advocate was not foreign to westerners. The French philosopher Maurice Merleau-Ponty in his book *Humanism and Terror* observed:

> In its own eyes Western humanism appears as the love of humanity, but for the rest of men it is only the custom and institution of a group of men, their password and occasionally their battle cry.
>
> ... Western humanism is a humanism of comprehension – a few mount guard around the treasure of Western culture; the rest are subservient ... it subordinates empirical humanity to a certain idea of man and its supporting institutions ... in the end Western humanism has nothing in common with a humanism in extension, which acknowledges in every man a power more precious than his productive capacity, not in virtue of being an organism endowed with such and such a talent, but as a being capable of self-determination and of situating himself in the world.[8]

It has become glaringly clear that embracing a definition of law and its rule that dispenses with ethics has produced immense suffering on human beings. Slavery, Nazism, and colonial and imperial wars are in part products of this separation. The suffering caused by this separation is not exclusively traceable to Euro-Westerners. Africans have played a role in bringing it about. It is a matter of historical record that after gaining their independence, some African nations gradually turned to authoritarianism and dictatorship causing much death and suffering on fellow Africans. We have witnessed Rwanda genocide, Darfur genocide, Liberia and Sierra Leone's genocides, and other instances of crimes against humanity and deprivation of human rights in other African regimes. The way that law and its rule have been defined has contributed to these horrors. Exclusion of ethics from the definition of law and its rule has provided an environment for the emergence and perpetuation of these horrors. To be sure, much depends on how ethics is defined. Ethics can be defined in a way that provides an environment for the emergence and perpetuation of these horrors.

African African legal ethicists are the architects of tomorrow's African cultural landscape, tomorrow's Africa, and tomorrow's cultured Africans. They are African culture workers. In carrying out this work, they are inevitably joined by other African ethicists, such as medical ethicists, political ethicists, and science and technology ethicists. It is the total conception and creation of the African that is at stake. They are agents of the re-Africanization of Africans and also agents of opening new dimensions of African social and cultural existence. The conception and the practice of law in Africa today must incorporate this agency and must be perceived as such by Africans. African African legal ethics must be understood dialectically. It is an ethics that must expose the ills of the current social and cultural existence and pave the way for an African social and cultural existence that is free of these ills. It must call attention to foreign contributors to these ills and, at the same time, be supportive of global efforts that seek to make the world a place where human dignity concretely pervades social and cultural existence.

Notes

1 John Locke, *The Second Treatise of Government*. New York: The Liberal Arts Press, 1952, p. 71.
2 Joseph Raz, *The Authority of Law: Essays on Law and Morality*. Oxford: Clarendon Press, 1979, p. 211.
3 Ibid, p. 211.
4 John Austin, *The Province of Law Determined*. Indianapolis, IN: Hackett, 1998, p. 184.

5 Carl Schmitt, *Political Theology*, trans. George Schwab. Chicago, IL: University of Chicago Press, 2005, p. 36.
6 See H.L.A. Hart's discussion of the "Separation of Law and Morals," *Harvard Law Review* 71(4): 593–629, 1958.
7 Martin Luther King, Jr. *Why we Can't Wait.* New York: Signet Books, 1964, p. 77.
8 Maurice Merleau-Ponty, *Humanism and Terror*, trans. John O'Neil. Boston. MA: Beacon Press, 1969, p. 176.

Chapter 5

African African legal ethics: a crisis of orientation

One who recognizes all men as members of his own body
Is a sound man to guard them[1]

Lao Tzu

The quote above is a part of ancient Chinese wisdom. On a reflection on African African legal ethics, it may be tempting to think of this quote as diversionary or as disorientating since it comes across as diverting attention from African African legal ethics. Diversion and disorientation are terms that bear multiple senses. They are cyphers that require ontological and existential deciphering. Lawyers and ethicists do not have a monopoly of deciphering them. The key to deciphering them is in the hands of every human being. They point to what is human in every human being. Attention to Chinese wisdom by an African is not necessarily a diversion or disorientating when what is at stake is African African legal ethics. One may be under an erroneous impression that Chinese wisdom has nothing to do with African wisdom or that African wisdom has nothing to do with Chinese wisdom. Wisdom is not the property of an individual or of a segment of the human community. It cannot be owned or monopolized. It is not an invention of this or that individual or an invention of this or that group of human beings. It is not an individual or group discovery. It cannot be copyrighted. It is a part of human heritage not because UNESCO declared it as such but because it is inherently as such. It is to be sharply distinguished from knowledge. Knowledge can be credited to this or that individual or group of individuals. Wisdom is not subject to such credit. Credit belongs to the human community.

An informed opinion on the location of wisdom must be grounded on the understanding of the geography of wisdom. Such geography cannot be determined unless it is first determined what wisdom is. What is wisdom is determined by its geography and what is its geography is determined by wisdom. In making either determination, one should be aware of the distinction between the geography of wisdom and the physical or the scientists' geography. The determination of former geography is the central concern of philosophy. A philosopher is in a better position to determine this geography for he or she is said to be a lover of wisdom. One is in a better position to determine what one truly loves if one recognizes what one loves. In addition, it is worth bearing in mind that a philosophical determination is not an end in itself. One seeks to determine what philosophy is in order to live wisely. To this extent, philosophy is a matter of ethics. Ethics is more than a branch of philosophy. It is at the core of what philosophy is. At this core, one seeks not only the knowledge of ethics, but also how this knowledge can lead to the kind of living that befits a human being. The objective in the investigation of African African legal ethics is to find out how one ought to lead an ethical life under the law, or differently stated, how one is to lead a life of law that is informed by ethics.

The determination of the soundness of a sound man – a man who ought to guard men – is a determination of a man who has a true grasp of ethics. Guarding men is the fundamental task of legal ethics and it is a task that is predicated on a proper grasp of what a sound human being is. Lao Tzu reminds us that such a man is a man who recognizes all men as members of his body. One cannot be reminded of what is not within oneself. Within oneself is the original site of legal ethics. It is a within oneself which is at the same time an outside of oneself, for one is what one is by outing oneself. Such a mode of being is preeminently ethical. The body that is subject to ethics has an ontological status that differs radically from a biophysical body. It is a legal-ethical body. The body is a body of all human beings. Anyone who does not recognize his or her body as the body of all human beings, or who does not recognize the bodies of all other human beings as his or her body is not a sound man. He or she does not understand his or her own body or the bodies of others. And he or she is not fit to guard all men, and because he is man among all men, he is unfit to guard himself.

The Euro-Western man has demonstrated that he is not sound and, as such, he is unfit to guard all men and is also unfit to guard himself. He does not understand his own body as the bodies of other men or the bodies of other men as his body. His relation to Africans serves as an example of this lack of understanding. The racist attitude he has adopted towards Africans indicates that he does not understand himself and he does not understand Africans. He does not recognize Africans as members of his own body and does not recognize the bodies of Africans as his own body. Relative to other human bodies, a human body is not self-enclosed. As a human body, it is open to other human bodies as a way of being itself. As a racist, the Euro-Western man sought to enclose himself within his own body and, at the same time, sought to enclose the African within his own body, thereby doing violence to both bodies. He sought to transform what is self-enclosed into what is not self-enclosed. He referred to his own body as White and referred to the African's body as Black and sought to erect an impregnable steel wall between the two bodies. His concept of all men excluded Africans as well as other non-Euro-Western people. It is exclusively made up of white men and incidentally, white women. It is this kind of thinking that has governed his sense of law and its rule that has governed his sense of ethics for more than the last five centuries.

This thinking and governance have been reinforced or, perhaps have been a product of a Judeo-Christian theology and religion. Judeo-Christianity professes to have a monopoly of truth about law, about ethics, and about what it is to be a human being. Its Muslim kin shares this profession. This profession is also reinforced by the prevailing view of philosophy in the Euro-West. A sound African Africans legal ethicist has to say categorically no to this profession, not only for his own sake but also for the sake of all human beings; for the sake of Euro-Westerners too. He or she is not to understand Lao Tzu as referring exclusively to Chinese. To assume that he was exclusively referring to Chinese is to assume that he was not a sound man. It is to assume that he did not know what he was talking about. Chinese as well as non-Chinese belong to a common human community. All human beings have a common human body and those who understand that have a sound mind and can guard human beings. It is all human beings that must be recognized as members of one's body. In seeing one's body one must see the bodies of all human beings. It is this seeing that is sound and that is a prerequisite for guarding all men. Africans, Chinese, and everyone else must be bound by this insight if legal ethics is to prevail in the domain of human beings.

The temptation to believe that when an African African legal ethicist acknowledges the truthfulness of the Chinese wisdom he or she is being diverted or disoriented from African wisdom is unlikely to arise when the same charge is levelled against an African African ethicist who acknowledges the Euro-Western contribution to his or her understanding of legal ethics. If it is unlikely to arise, it is because the African African legal ethicist has been held hostage in Euro-Western understanding of legal ethics. As indicated earlier, the conventional understanding of philosophy and its history in the Euro-West has propagated the view that indigenous Africa is devoid of philosophy and an African who takes an interest in philosophy must be oriented to the Euro-West. Accordingly, if an African African legal ethics is to have a philosophical foundation it must be oriented to the Euro-West. It must be grounded in the Euro-Western conception of philosophy. Today, it appears that conventional understanding of philosophy falls within this conception of philosophy. Indeed, this appears to be evidenced by philosophy in African universities. The philosophy curriculum in these universities is largely an imitation of the philosophy curriculum in the Euro-West. In the context of this curriculum, a philosophical study of African legal ethics turns out to be mainly guided by the Euro-Western philosophical canon. This is a very conservative canon. It radically dismisses, ignores, and rejects any and all other canons. Any other canon is pure nonsense. An African African philosopher who rejects this canon is institutionally silenced. The very idea of an African African philosophical canon is ridiculous. As a prisoner of the Euro-Western canon the African is not only ignorant of his or her African canon, he or she is shut off from familiarity with other non-Euro-Western philosophical canons. It is not accidental at all that little is known about African philosophy in African universities or that little is known about Chinese or Asian philosophy. In the area of legal ethics and in the area of ethics in general, what one often hears is Euro-Western ethicists or Euro-Western branches of ethics. Although it is not as fashionable as it used to be, the underlying message is that the African is a bushman, a savage, or a primitive whose thinking is not only unphilosophical but also anti-philosophical. Chinese and other Asians and, in general, most of the other non-Euro-Western peoples have been pressured to adopt this Euro-Western perception of Africans. Today, it is difficult for non-Africans to see Africans without the mediation of racist Euro-Western lenses. Even Africans are yet to be immunized from seeing through these lenses. If an African is to find his or her way back to an African African seeing of legal ethics, he or she must radically change his or her orientation. Finding his or her way back does not entail being cut off from other human beings, if only because to be cut off from other human beings is to be cut off from oneself. He or she must recognize himself or herself in others and must recognize others in himself or in herself.

It should be clear that what has been said so far about African African legal ethics is mostly a reaction to the regime of legal ethics that has been imposed on Africans by the Euro-West and by Muslims. Although no legal ethics can be solely based on a reaction to an external imposition if it is to have its integrity, a reaction is necessitated if to assert itself there is a need to remove an obstacle that stands in the way. The historical situation in which Africans find themselves calls for such a necessity. The colonial experience and the apartheid experience to which Africans have been subjected cannot be wished away. It is an act of bad faith for anyone to pretend that the experience is inconsequential in addressing African African legal ethics. In partial recognition of this necessity, South Africa adopted what has been referred to as a transformative Constitution – a Constitution that calls for transformative legal ethics. The drafters of this Constitution recognized the harm that apartheid had caused and contained provisions recognizing the harm and the remedy that was required. But for all the praised it has received, it remains primarily a product of Euro-Western neoliberalism. This means that the Euro-Western conception of law and Euro-Western conception of ethics, for the most part, prevailed. In short, Euro-Western legal ethics prevailed. Like a large portion of the rest of Africa, South Africa remained oriented to the Euro-West and not to Africa. The Euro-West continued to be the location of the oasis of law and the oasis of ethics. Africans were presented as having no seeds of law or seeds of ethics. They had to get these seeds from the Euro-West. They even had to import soil for planting these seeds for African soil did not have the requisite nutrients for the growing of these seeds. Judeo-Christianity mediated by the Euro-West has continued to be the source of ethics. The common law tradition and the civil law tradition continue to guide the understanding of law and its practice. Africans are pressured not to import the seeds or the soil from other sources. In non-Christian Muslim Africa, a Muslim conception of law and legal practice prevails. Seeds of law and ethics are imports from Mecca and so is the soil for planting these seeds. There is enormous pressure not to import seeds or soil from other sources. The economy of law, as is the case with the economy of ethics, is dominated by non-Africans. Africans have been reduced to beggars of law and to beggars of ethics; thus, into beggars of legal ethics. They suffer from paternalism in legal ethics. This paternalism is a part of the general paternalism that African suffers from in other areas of their existence. It is precisely this deeply rooted and widespread paternalism that constitutes the crisis of orientation in legal ethics as it exists in Africa today. It is a crisis that is deeply rooted at the heart of being African.

If it is conceded that the African is oriented away from himself or herself in the prevailing conception of legal ethics, the African African legal ethics that is necessitated is one that reorients Africans – a cosmic revolution – more radical than a Copernican revolution. African African legal ethics ought to be an indispensable factor in this revolution. It is this revolution that must be at the center of the African African conception of law and of the African African conception of legal practice. African legal education must be a revolutionary education so that those who teach African law know what they are teaching so that those who seek legal education know what is expected of them, and those who end up practicing law know what they will be practicing. African law professors and African law practitioners must be in the service of this revolution. Instead of thinking that this is a task imposed from without, they should view it as self-serving. The self that is being served here is not the modern European self – a self that is isolated from other selves. It is not egocentric. An African self does not exist apart from other African selves. Its African well-being is the well-being of every African. Lest he misconceive himself or herself being truly conscious of himself or herself entails being conscious of being human. No human being is what he or she is in isolation from other human beings. One is human in communion with other human beings. African legal ethics embraces and affirms this insight. This insight brings into relief the kind of genuine and concrete universality that African African legal ethics embraces, affirms, and promotes. This is an indispensable foundation for an African African legal ethicist who seeks to engage with non-African legal ethicists in a genuine discourse on legal ethics. Consequently, the claim that an African African legal ethics be indigenously grounded does not seek to isolate an African legal ethicist from other legal ethicists. It provides him or her with a solid foundation from which he or she can engage with non-African ethicists. Moreover, he or she does not seek to dislocate non-Africans from their solid foundations. He or she is not a missionary of legal ethics. He or she meets others on a communal foundation where everyone one is what he or she is without preying on others, without engaging in anthropophagy. African African legal ethics puts a stop to those who seek to make Africans meet their dietary needs.

A truly African African legal ethics calls on Africans to be self-oriented; that is, to be oriented towards themselves. It is a process of homecoming. This does not imply that they have to be narcissistic or solipsistic. To be oriented towards themselves does not imply that they must turn away from other human beings. To turn away from other human beings is to turn away from themselves. They must affirm themselves and secure themselves in the human community for it is in such a community that they are what they are. This human home is recognized beyond the borders of Africa. From this community, there arises true jurisprudence and true ethics. This is where their legal ethics is at home. Legal ethics secures, and affirms all men in their human home. If African African legal ethics is true to itself this is its task. The same Chinese sage quoted previously says,

> There is no need to run outside
>
> For better seeing,
>
> Nor to peer from a window. Rather abide
>
> At the center of your being;
>
> For the more you leave it, the less you learn.
>
> Search your heart and see
>
> If he is wise who takes each turn:
>
> The way to do is to be.[2]

What is said here is not uniquely Chinese. It lies coiled in the heart of every human being. By forcefully being oriented towards the Euro-West, Africans have been deprived of this awareness. They have been deprived of the essential contact not only with themselves but also with Chinese and with other Asians. This essential contact is the oxygen of legal ethics. In essential human affairs – where legal ethics is embedded – there is no inside and there is no outside. To look inside is to look outside. This is the spatiality of being human.

> It cannot be, when the root is neglected, that what should spring from it will be well ordered. It never has been the case that what was of great importance has been slightly cared for, and, at the same time, that what was of slight importance has been greatly cared for.[3]

One finds the same sentiment in an observation made by Malcolm X, an American of African descent who recognized the significance of the root in the cultivation of self-knowledge and self-understanding. He said,

> Just as a tree without roots is dead, a people without history or cultural roots also becomes a dead people. And when you look at us, those of us who are called Negro, we're called that because we are like a dead people. We have nothing to identify ourselves as part of the human family. You know you can tell what kind of a tree it is by looking at the leaves. If the leaves are gone, you can look at the bark and tell what kind it is. But when you find a tree with leaves gone and the bark gone, everything gone, you call that what? A stump. And you cannot identify a stump as easily as you can identify a tree.[4]

For more than five centuries there has been a Euro-Western crusade to inculcate amnesia in Africans making them believe that their roots are other people's roots. Euro-Western legal ethics has played a major role in this crusade and on occasion a segment of Africans has aided his crusade. This segment has included disoriented and misguided African legal ethicists.

For almost six centuries, Africans have been subjected to a crusade of deracination. They have been pressured to orient themselves away from themselves, away from Africa. That is, they have been under pressure to uproot themselves from themselves and from Africa. What African African legal ethics calls for is an opposition to this uprooting orientation. Ultimately, it is an unparalleled cosmic revolution, perhaps more radical than a Copernican revolution. Legal education should have its primary task in preparing African students for such a revolution. Their professors cannot successfully prepare them if they themselves are not prepared for it. The need for their re-education is yet to be recognized.

Notes

1 Lao Tzu, *The Way of Life*, trans. Witter Bynner. New York: The Berkeley Group, 1994, p. 43.
2 Ibid., p. 75.
3 Confucius, *The Great Learning*. http://classics.mit.edu/Confucius/learning.html, accessed October 9, 2019.
4 Malcolm X, *On Afro-American History*. New York: Pathfinder Press, 1990, p. 25.

Conclusion

The last time I saw my mother – the time before she passed away – I sat next to her. Between us, there was a moment of pregnant silence, perhaps calling attention to the fact that we did not know what to say to each other. I was about to return to my adopted country – the county of my residence. There was a silence pervaded by anxiety. None of us appeared sure of what would be born out of this silence. A midwife was not present to assist in giving birth to speech, and it appeared that even if there were one, assistance would be futile. After a few minutes, which appeared to be eternity, she looked at me and said, "The sun is setting." I knew right away what she meant. She was more than a hundred years old. I was about to leave not knowing whether we would ever see each other again. I was working and living thousands of miles away in a country she never visited and that she would never visit. She knew nothing about the country of my residence other than the fact that her son and his family were living there. She knew that the country was called America, but she had no idea where this country was or what it really was. As I looked at her, and as she looked at me, our eyes were avoiding contact with each other. In Africa, it is unusual and impolite for younger people to look directly at the eyes of their elders, especially their parents. Out of respect, the younger look down to avoid eye contact. In matters that are truly important or when a younger person is being scolded, chastised, or admonished, he or she is asked by an elder or by a parent to have eye contact. None of these applied at the final moment between my mother and me. We did not look at each other, but we knew that both of us were fully present to each other. We did not have to look at each other to recognize our presence to each other. Parental relation gave way without giving way. Its place was taken over by a rare dread. It was clear that although we were sitting next to each other, there was an unbridgeable gap between us – a gap that, at any time, would absolutely be beyond the possibility of being bridged. This gap was filled by dread. Indeed, for my mother, the sun was setting. For me, the sun would inevitably set too, but it seemed to me that it would be long after her sunset. I felt full of youthfulness. Thinking or even imagining my sunset did not concretely register in my consciousness. But in a sense, this was not my time. It was my mother's time. It was her sunset. To be sure, at the time, it was also my time too – an awkward time since I could not clearly distinguish my mother's time from my time. There was an uncanny blending of times. I was overwhelmed by the possibility of never ever seeing her alive again and by her never ever seeing me again.

Everyone has his or her own sunset. My mother never lived and could not have lived to see her sunset. Every one of us is deprived of seeing his or her own sunset. Sunset "concludes" life. We are haunted by what comes after this "conclusion." We are shut off for eternity from what comes after the "conclusion." To be sure, this does not preclude the power to imagine. However, imagination is imagination; nothing more.

What is being claimed about the sunset applies to the sunrise. Reflecting on pre-sunrise appears equally enigmatic, equally imaginary. One was not before one was. How one was before one was does not appear to be a preoccupation for many of us, for what often troubles us is what is to come after sunset, after we are no more. Regarding post-sunset, many of us are filled with anxiety. Such anxiety does not exist in pre-sunrise. In either case, we are not able to contrast a pre-sunrise state with a post-sunset state. If the poles of this in-between (life) are constituted by non-being, what is one to make of life? Must life itself not be inevitably and inescapably haunted by non-being? But how can life (the in-between) lie between two non-beings? What is one to make of the between-ness – a between-ness that is separated by non-beings? Is there any going from and going to which is other than coming from nowhere and going to nowhere? It is this in-between that we call life. It is what constitutes the soil out of which law grows and, at the same time, the soil out of which ethics grows. In short, this is the birthplace of legal ethics. Law and ethics are about life, about this in-between. Both seek to regulate it for our own good. But they cannot do so intelligently without understanding what they are regulating, or without a grasp of the good that is aimed at by what they seek to regulate. Conventional wisdom leads us to believe that law and ethics are about rules. But rules in either case are unintelligible without understanding what is ruled, without understanding life and its demands. Often, when we try to make sense of legal ethics, we are oblivious of life; we rarely see it as a key to the understanding of life, as the embodiment of life. There is no legal ethics in pre-sunrise and there is no legal ethics in post-sunset. Legal ethics is about the in-between. It is the key to the in-between. It is a key to life, and life is a key to it. It is in the service of life.

It will not come as a surprise if the question is raised about the relevance of what I have said about my mother's affecting presence. It is reasonable to ask, "What is its relevance to the conclusion of a small book on Africanizing legal ethics?" What has been said about my mother's pending sunset to do with African African legal ethics? It is tempting to set aside what transpired between my mother and me, or to take it as a digression that is inconsequential to law, to ethics, and to legal ethics. It is too personal or too intimate to bear significantly on law, ethics, and on legal ethics. Unlike what transpired between my mother and me, the prevailing wisdom is that law is impersonal and that we ought not to have an intimate relation with it, and ethics is nothing more than a body of principles to live by. It is in the light of this conventional wisdom that a lawyer is expected to set aside his or her personal or conventional ethics when he or she is thinking or acting like a lawyer. It is precisely this coldhearted understanding of law and legal ethics that led to the insensitivity of legal practitioners to the Nazi regime, to the enslavement and colonization of Africans. It is what anesthetizes legal practitioners to the cruelty of apartheid and to racist or dictatorial regimes in Africa and elsewhere. It shields lawyers from ethical/moral accountability to citizens. It anesthetizes professors of law, judges, lawyers, magistrates, and those who are called upon to administer law. In colonial situations, under the cover of the distinction between personal/conventional ethics and legal ethics, colonizers were able to impose their inhumane social and cultural values under the guise of legal ethics. Apparently, personal ethics is severed from public ethics enabling one to uphold oneself personally as ethical while being indifferent to ethics in the public arena. Nurturing this severance is the diet that is conventionally fed to law students by law professors in the Euro-West. It is how one is trained to be a lawyer. The distinction between personal and public ethics in legal ethics is not as clear as it is made out to be. It is societal and culture specific. It is not to be assumed that it is universal. It is a political construction of law and a political construction of ethics. Legal ethics is inescapably political.

Whether what I have said about the affecting presence of my mother is or is not relevant to what has been said about African African legal ethics has much to do with how one understands law and how one understands ethics. How one understands either is a matter of how one is socially and culturally situated historically. This situatedness has everything to do with what a human being is. All that has been said or on what can be said about being human in African African legal ethics has not been said and will never be said by me or by anyone else. It is dauntingly open. Accordingly, the sunset my mother and I were contemplating could be construed as analogous to a conclusion to this book. I cannot position myself after the conclusion, for the conclusion is yet to be concluded. I am on this side of it and will never consciously be on the other side of it. I cannot say I have concluded this book or that I am concluding it. To say so is to position myself ahead of it and, in doing so, I would not have concluded it, and I would not be concluding it. Essential conclusions are imaginary. They are horizonal. Nothing more or less should be asked of a book on African African legal ethics. African African legal ethics is about being African – a being that is what it is by being ahead of itself. It is also an ethics that intrinsically touches all of us in so far as we are human. African African ethics cannot be truly what it is if it sets Africans apart from other human beings. It is a call to preempt such separateness. To this extent, it is a universal legal ethics.

This little book is a journey – a journey whose beginning cannot be pinpointed. Its sunrise is unthinkable. It is purely imaginary. Its sunset (conclusion) is equally unthinkable and is purely imaginary. Does every journey have to come to an end? Maybe, maybe not. It all depends on the kind of journey that one has in mind. In our case, it depends on what kind of a journey is African legal ethics. Let us think of Africa legal ethics as a journey. To be what it is, it is a journey that we must take together – not as outsiders but as our innermost journey. It is our journey. It is a journey about us, about our lives. We are it – whether we are or are not Africans. It is a journey that teaches us what and who we are. If we are to be taught what or who we are, we are such that we do not know what or who we are; at least, not fully. Law is about us and so is ethics. In short, legal ethics is about us. It is so even if we are or are not qualified as Africans.

As a human being, an African is not foreign to other human beings. Similarly, other human beings are not foreign to what it is to be an African. Moreover, we are what or who we are by being ahead of ourselves. We are not fully ourselves, and how this is the case we do not fully know, and we will never fully know. Properly understood, legal ethics (African or non-African) instills and sustains this mode of consciousness. So far, what has been said has already taken us to the neighborhood of the journey that is our being – the neighborhood of our being. Although we have moved, we are where we began, and we are moving towards where we began, and to where we are. To move otherwise is to abandon ourselves as human beings. Wherever human beings go, they cannot leave themselves behind. This is an *Ubuntu* journey – a journey from being human to being human.

As indicated previously, the African, law, and ethics and hence, African African legal ethics are horizontal. Each has a border that is still to be defined or that is provisionally defined. This being the case, a conclusion that is appropriate to this work is inconclusive and must be so. It preserves us in the journey we have undertaken and that we are still taking. In a sense, we are where we began, sort of; sort of in the sense that we have moved. We have moved without moving. This is the enigma of language, the enigma of thinking; ultimately, the enigma of life. To be what one is to be at a distance to what one is. The distance cannot be eliminated. Writing or speaking about African African legal ethics is an endless task.

What has been said about African African legal ethics is not intended to have an empirical grounding – a grounding that would tempt one to look for empirical validation of what has been said. If it had an empirical grounding, it would be a grounding that is not stationary, a metastable grounding. It would be a grounding that is on the move. Human social existence in which legal ethics is situated does not stand still. It is historical. It has a past that remains to be explored and that informs the present. It has a present pregnant with a past and that is pregnant with a future. It has a future that is itself pregnant with futures. It has a grounding that is not subject to empirical validation. It is open-ended. To seek such a validation is to do violence to it. How can one seek validation of oneself as a human being without making a mockery of such seeking? As features of human social existence, law, ethics, and, hence, legal ethics, are subject to what prevails in such existence. Each one of them is open-ended. Necessarily, what can be said about them is inconclusive. It is ongoing. This also applies to what is to be understood as being African. The African of today is not entirely an African of today. In part, he or she is an African of yesterday and an African of tomorrow and the day after tomorrow. What is said about him or her defies closure. He or she is in the making. The African is the possibility of being African. Precisely for this reason, what is said of him or of her is not subject to empirical verification. Ortega y Gasset, a Spanish philosopher, has correctly asserted that man is a novelist of himself. To be a novelist of oneself is to make oneself what one is; it is to maintain the distance between what one is and what one is. The same can be said about the African or about any other human being. What is said about being African, about law, and about ethics applies to African African legal ethics. Nothing about legal ethics can be said definitively since it is in the process of becoming without ever ceasing to become. African African legal ethics is novelistic and the understanding that is proper to it is equally novelistic.

It cannot be denied that Africa is a continent. It is a geographical territory, but it is also more than a geographical territory. African legal ethics opens an Africa that is more than geographical – an Africa that is a novel. Africa is a novel in the making. It cannot be denied that Africa is not politically, culturally, or societally united and to speak of legal ethics that spans the entire continent strikes one as nonsensical. How then can one speak meaningfully of African African legal ethics as if there were one legal ethics covering the entire continent and that is embraced by all Africans? What would appear to make sense is to speak of legal ethics in Africa, and then select a small portion of Africa, a certain portion of Africans (what Euro-Westerners call a tribe), and then focus on the legal ethics in it. Let it be admitted that this is a legitimate concern – a concern about what has been said in this small book. In the light of this concern, the legitimacy of this conclusion is thereby put in question. If the legitimacy of this concern is recognized, it must be fully recognized. To be fully recognized, the legitimacy of this concern should be raised. Legitimacy is multiple. We get from it what we put into it. There are presuppositions of what Africa is and presuppositions of who Africans are. For example, there is a modern European Africa and there are modern European Africans. This modern European Africa is not African Africa and the modern European Africans are not African Africans. Moreover, modern European Africa can be replaced by another European Africa and modern European Africans can be replaced by other European Africans. Similarly, African Africans have their own modern Africa and they have their own modern African Africans. The conventional non- or anti-African modern Africa and the conventional non- or anti-African modern African can be replaced by a modern African Africa and by a modern African African. African African legal ethics is a part of this historic replacement. Nothing is definitive about it. It is not cast in stone. The African, as is the case with every other being, is an open being. African African legal ethics is about this openness. It is constituted and disclosed in this openness and as this openness.

Africa is open-ended, and so is every one of its expressions. For example, this is how the African Union is to be understood. As it exists today, what is referred to as the African Union is aspirational. It is an ideal. Today, there is no question about the fact that Africa is largely a mosaic of cultures, societies, and nations – all of which are open-ended. Or as it is commonly said by Euro-Westerners, Africa is a mosaic of ethnic groups – groups that even today are inappropriately referred to as tribes. And it cannot also be denied that within each of them, there are pluralities. How then can one speak about African legal ethics as if there were one legal ethics shared by all Africans? Isn't such a concept empty – a concept without content? If the concept of African African legal ethics is to have content, should it not be decentralized so that it can refer to each of the aggregates into which Africans are grouped, i.e., nations, or ethnic groups? This way of thinking takes us on a path that may be erroneous. This becomes a genuine possibility if we bear in mind that being African is the possibility of being African. To give an African the sense of being African, he or she does not have to be circumscribed. There is nothing to circumscribe. If it is accepted that the African as a human being is a novelist of himself or herself, he or she is free to constitute himself or herself and cannot be held captive to this or that ethnic group or to this or that national group. Let it not be forgotten that, today, African national identities – identities with which Africans associate themselves, are of recent origin. African national jurisdictions are constructs. There was a time when they did not exist and there may come a time when they will not exist, or when they will be replaced by different boundaries. It is also to be borne in mind that ethnic groups are volatile. Their borders are not hermetically sealed. However they are constituted, African groupings are not bound to be eternally the way they are constituted today. Even in current groupings, African African legal ethics can be construed in ways that transcend the manner it is currently constituted. Moreover, there is no African group that is what it is in isolation from other African groups. This is not so simply because each one of them is located in the continent of Africa, but because each one is African. And, in being so, they share Africanness. This shared Africanness is in the process of becoming what it is. That is, it is in the process of being constituted. It is not an empirical concept. What is shared is the possibility of being African and a possibility remains perennially a possibility – becoming without ever becoming.

If it is recognized that African union is aspirational, and if it is recognized that the course of its being is the course of being African, it should not be assumed that all Africans are in support of this process, or that they are aware of what is at stake in this process. It is undeniable that there are Africans who seek to lock themselves up in their ethnic (tribal), religious, political, cultural class and national enclaves and, in some cases, they are encouraged to pursue this path by non-Africans. They view African union as a threat to their identity and to their interests. They view an attempt to constitute as unified a sense of being African as a threat. They would and find it offensive to entertain an African legal ethics that would be in the service of African union or in the service of constituting a unified sense of being African. By African African legal ethics, they understand African national legal ethics, and even this understanding, is itself broken down into particularities that make up the nation or that make up the society in which they live. A legal ethics that does not recognize the sanctity of the existing sovereignty of the enclaves in which they reside is taken to be abstract or a utopian idea that is irresponsive to their immediate needs. They would like to see African African legal ethics subjected to decentralization or to devolution. They would like to embrace a legal ethics that is ethno-ethics. This is mooted as democratic legal ethics at the grass root, as true democracy where "people" are truly shaping their destiny. Euro-Western missionaries and Euro-Western professors of this democracy invade Africa in droves to secure and promote the legitimacy of these processes and to falsely inculcate in Africans the belief that Euro-Western societies are prosperous and bearers of human dignity and human rights due to the belief that they have embraced democracy. What these missionaries and professors and have in mind is a liberal society. In legal ethics, what they seek to promote is liberal legal ethics. Their intention is to transform or to constitute African African legal ethics into liberal legal ethics. They aim at presenting African legal ethics as parasitic to Euro-Western legal ethics, at presenting African African legal ethics as an imitation of Euro-Western legal ethics. Africa becomes Africa as construed in Euro-Western imagination, African jurisprudence as an imitation of Euro-Western jurisprudence, and African ethics as an imitation of Euro-Western ethics. Moreover, as has been pointed out, if legal ethics is ultimately a window to what it is be a human being, African legal ethics becomes a window to the view of being human that is an imitation of what is understood as a human being in the Euro-West. African legal ethics exposes and seeks to erase the parasitism of the conception of being African that is attributed to the African by Euro-Westerners. To accomplish this task, it must be grounded on an indigenous African African legal ethics that is grounded on a conception of being human that is indigenous to Africans. This indigeneity is not in a calabash waiting to be dished out. It is not to be viewed as a fossil that must be dug out and exhibited or passed around by ethno-anthropologists. It remains to be worked out and it must be an ongoing process. Moreover, being African consists of becoming African and, if an African is African, he or she will inescapably be ahead of himself or herself as a way of being himself or herself. African legal ethics is an ethics of African union. It is a uniting ethics. It ingathers Africans. It seeks to bring Africans home, where they are constituted as Africans. To take it seriously is to take African union seriously. The realization or the inspiration of either is the realization or the inspiration of the other. Both realization and inspiration are the realization and inspiration of being African; ultimately the inspiration and realization of being human. Here no human being is stranger.

In the light of what is claimed above, an understanding of African African legal ethics is not fully exhausted when placed in a professional world. No profession exists in a societal vacuum. There is a societal ethics that forms the basis for every professional ethics. African professional legal ethics is not an exception. The societal ethics that constitutes this basis is where professional ethics draws its inspiration. Societal ethics has a tomorrow and the day after tomorrow. It does not stand still. Societies are not fungible. They differ in their ethics and in what inspires their professional ethics. The differences are not in opposition to or ought to be in opposition to each other, if only because they are all bound to being human. Differences in the conception of being human cannot entirely be such that each excludes the others for then they would not be human. Ultimately, what is human binds them. Each legal ethics acquires legitimacy as legal ethics by being bound to this human bond. This bond is to be worked out ceaselessly. It is historical. A mummified legal ethics is preposterous. Societal transformation brings about transformation of legal ethics and legal ethics itself brings about societal transformation. Shifting aspects of societal ethics are attended by shifting aspects of legal ethics. To survive, societies need breathing space and this applies to societal ethics as well as professional ethics. If legal ethics is societal ethics it must be perennially a transitional ethics.

Every professional ethics ultimately is accountable to the society in which it exists. It is ultimately accountable to all members of the society in which it exists. This accountability is not exclusively reserved for those in the legal profession. Every citizen is a guardian of legal ethics because he or she is a guardian of societal ethics in the society in which he or she lives. Ultimately, this is a guardianship of oneself as a social being – a mode of being that makes a human being a human being. Moreover, because every society is a member of human society, one cannot truly engage in self-guardianship without guarding every other human being. Human societies do not solely form an aggregate in human community. They have an organic relationship with each other. There is what is African in each and every non-African and there is what is non-African in each and every African. If this were not the case, it would be meaningless to refer to ourselves as human. Affirming and pursuing this mode of being ought to be at the heart of African African legal ethics and also at the heart of every other legal ethics. It ought to be at the heart of all the branches of ethics and at the heart of ethics itself. Ethics is a window to what a human being is, and this entails being a window to the well-being of a human being.

African African legal ethics is not what it is by denying the cosmopolitan or universal legal ethics. It is compatible with either version of legal ethics. All it insists on is that either of these versions of legal ethics be grounded locally. A cosmopolitan legal ethics – an ethics that is truly universal – becomes so from a local standpoint. It is such a standpoint that has been denied by the prevailing version of Euro-Western legal ethics. The Euro-Western version of cosmopolitan legal ethics has been and still is a version of local legal ethics that has been illicitly universalized and imposed on Africans and on other non-western people. This has taken place under cover of reason or under cover of the neutrality or impartiality of law and its rule. Universality by imposition is not truly universal. Moreover, as has been pointed out previously, since legal ethics leads to and is founded on the sense of being human, there are no general cosmopolitan or universal human beings. One is a human being locally, concretely. Imposed humanness dehumanizes. No human being or group of human beings has a monopoly of the blueprint of what it is to be a human being. Genuine legal ethics demands that we behave and think in a way that exemplifies a singular mode of being human – a singularity that exemplifies the universality of being human. It is this mode of being human that animates African African legal ethics. The depth and range of this animation is yet to be fully recognized and implemented. To be fully recognized and implemented it must inform every aspect of societal existence. Law is not a monopoly of lawyers and ethics is not a monopoly of ethicists. Law and ethics (legal ethics) are the flesh of society. Both must run through the veins and the capillaries of every member of society, both individually and communally. In the light of this sense of legal ethics, we are able to undertake a critique of the legal ethics of law school and the legal ethics of the practitioners of law.

One may surmise that it is not ethics that is the primary focus in legal education and in legal practice. It may be a speculation but with some justification that it is not a concern with ethics that drives young men and young women to law school. For the most part, today, attraction to law school is driven by a craving for wealth, power, and for societal status. I do not want to give the erroneous impression that it is only in the legal profession where this happens. Most likely, there is this element in all professions. It is indeed the case that, in modern society, one needs to have a means of income to survive. Above all, one needs some food and shelter. However, we should not forget that hunger, a part of modern hunger, is a product of the way that society is organized. It could be a product of a legal system and a product of the legal education carried out within society by blessings of law and by prevailing lawyers' ethics. In Africa, many are hungry because the legal establishment is either corrupt or turns a blind eye to corruption. The economic injustice and social degradation of some members of society takes place with the blessing of the legal system. In part, this is a result of the deficiency of legal education – an education that does not instill concern with communal societal justice in law students. Professors of law and the administrators of law schools are partly responsible for this state of affairs. It should not be forgotten that for Africans, a human society is more than human. It does not only encompass the living, the dead, and the unborn. It also encompasses the not-human – not by reducing it to the human but by transcending the human-non-human divide.

Years ago, I heard an African student from Namibia tell an American audience that he was not confident in answering the question from Americans when they asked him how he was. He told the audience that where he comes from, were he to be asked how he was, one possible answer would be that he was not well. He added that when a member of his family was not well, when his relative was not well, when his friend or his neighbor was not well, how could he be well? If one of his animals or his chickens was not well, how could he be well? If his neighbors were at old with each other or the neighboring communities had a quarrel among themselves, how could he say he was well? If his crops were not doing well because of the shortage of rain, how could he say that he was well? If all was well, he could then say he was well; otherwise he was not well.

The view taken by the Namibian student is illustrative of what lies at the heart of African African legal ethics. Ethics has everything do with environmentally being well, with holistic well-being. When well-being bears on law, or when law bears on ethics, we have here legal ethics. Well-being is the center of legal ethics and, from this center both law and ethics get their charge. It is from this center that they are illuminated and in which they become what they are. The well-being that is at stake here is more than human well-being. It is more than humanistic well-being. It is an environmental well-being. As an ethics it embraces all that is. Human well-being is a part of this comprehensive well-being. Differently stated, the well-being of human beings is inextricably bound to the well-being of every being – not just fellow human beings, but all beings. Hence, ultimately, legal ethics is not anthropomorphic or anthropocentric. This claim appears to be contrary to the long-standing belief in the Euro-West that man is the center of ethics. Clearly, what we learn from the history of Euro-Western ontology, above all other beings a human being is privileged, and both legal ethics and ethics in general are anthropocentric. The imperial dominance of this Eurocentric anthropology and of the legal ethics that is a part of it poses as serious an obstacle on the way to understanding African anthropology and the legal ethics that arises from it.

Leo Strauss, an eminent thinker in the Euro-Western world, has observed that, "Western man became what he is and is what he is through the coming together of the Biblical faith and Greek thought" and adds, "in order to understand ourselves and to illuminate our trackless way into the future, we must understand Jerusalem and Athens."[1] By "ourselves", Strauss has in mind Euro-Westerners, and understands Euro-Westerners to represent the highest expression of what it is to be truly human. Judeo-Christianity has played a major role in the construction of this hegemonic humanism. The belief that Euro-Westerners are God's chosen people lies deeply in Euro-Western self-conception, in European humanism. It should not come as a surprise that this God is a Euro-Western God – a God disguised as a God for all – a God for both Euro-Westerners and non-Euro-Westerners.

In this statement, perhaps unintentionally, Strauss omits the Romans. It is undeniable that Romans have contributed significantly to the construction of the Euro-Western man's identity. This is particularly important because the Romans have played a major role in the foundation of Euro-Western humanism. It should not be forgotten that Greek thought was not European, and the Greeks were not Europeans, and the Romans were not Europeans. Equally, biblical faith was not a European faith. The architects of this faith were non-Europeans. Consequently, one can surmise that since Europeans have not made a case regarding what is unique about their identity, they derive their identity from being parasitic to the Greeks, to the Romans, to the biblical faith people (the descendants of Adam). In other words, western man does not have an ancestor of his own. He is a product of parasitism. He is a parasite who denies his parasitism. He has an addiction to the Greeks, to the Romans, and to the descendants of Adam. He is a homeless man who seeks a home in other people's homes. Although he is a stranger to Athens and to Jerusalem, he has *invaded* these two cities and has sought to make himself at home in them. He is a squatter who, after several centuries, has established himself as true owner of these cities. He appears to be a man in flight from himself and who seeks to avoid coming face to face with the lack of being in his own being. He has transformed the parasitism to which he is subject into a crusade – a crusade in which he seeks to convert non-westerners into believing that they too are homeless in their home and that they should be like he is or what he has become, or at least an imitation of what he has become or of what he is; in short, to become a parasite of a parasite or an imitation of an imitation. When the cowrie shells are cast on the divination board what they reveal is that the Euro-Western man's legal ethics is a part of this crusade. One of the primary victims of this crusade is the African. As Frantz Fanon has noted,

> For colonialism, this vast continent was a den of savages, infested with superstitions and fanaticism, destined to be despised, cursed by God, a land of cannibals, a land of "niggers". Colonialism's condemnation is continental in scale, Colonialism's claims that the precolonial period was akin to a darkness of the human soul refers to the entire continent of Africa. The colonized endeavors to rehabilitate himself and escape the sting of colonialism, obey the same rules of logic.[2]

African African legal ethics is a means of rehabilitating this conception of Africa. It is a rehabilitation that seeks to restore the primal human community in which all human beings are members. It is worth repeating that an African cannot be an African in isolation from other Africans. Moreover an African cannot be human in isolation from other human beings. No human being can be human in isolation from other human beings. This too is a central message in African African legal ethics. This is not simply a reaction to colonialism. It is what one is as an African and as a human being. As is commonly said in Africa, "we are, therefore, I am." This is said not to deny individuality but to affirm individuality that is truly human. Individuality outside of the human community is symptomatic of severe madness.

From a Euro-Western perspective, if an African is to be human, he or she must cease to be African and become a parasite of a parasite – the parasite of the Euro-Western man. He or she must disavow his or her African ancestors and attach himself or herself to the western man – the man who has disavowed his ancestor and attached himself to other men's ancestors – a man who has allowed himself to be adopted by the Greeks, by the Romans, and Adam's descendants. African African legal ethics sensitizes Africans to this pernicious and perverse humanism. It is protective of the African's primordial, non-derivative and non-parasitical mode of being African. A conclusion that befits a work of African

African legal ethics – a work of ethics that is truly and genuinely African, has this as its mission: calling the African into the consciousness of being African in a non-derivative and non-parasitic sense. It is a homecoming for African. This sense of African African legal ethics is yet to fully register in the consciousness of African students of African African legal ethics. What is also yet to fully register in the consciousness of these students is that by African students it is meant all Africans and not solely the African students in the legal academy. To do its duty, the African legal academy is to be Africanized – Africanized in a way that makes every African a student of legal ethics whether or not she or he is associated with the legal academy. An African African legal ethics is an ethics of African society. When it is transformed solely into an academic ethics, it ceases to be what it is.

In an address to fellow Europeans, Nietzsche, a German philosopher, has observed that, "The democratization of Europe is at the same time an involuntary arrangement for the cultivation of tyrants – taking that word in every sense, including the most spiritual."[3] The democratization of Europe that Nietzsche speaks about includes the institutionalization of law as well as the institutionalization of ethics. Democracy produces a law and an ethics that is unique to it. Or, it produces a law and an ethics that gives it legitimacy. If Nietzsche is right, it can be reasonably assumed that the cultivation of tyrants has been the product of a particular institutionalization of legal ethics. Clearly, this is not what conventionally is expected of democracy, of law, or of ethics under democracy. In conventional wisdom it is expected that democratization is an antidote to the rise of the tyrants. This antidote takes the form of law and the form of ethics. The question is whether, in reference to Europe, Nietzsche is right. To determine whether he is right one must look at what has become of Europe, at what Europe has made of itself. To do so, it is appropriate to pay attention to the book that has guided the construction of its identity: the Christian Bible. Europe has presented itself to itself and to the world as Christian and when it poses as secular, the secularism is Christian. The New Testament, part of the Christian Bible contains a criterion for truth, for knowledge. It is said by Matthew of the Gospels, "Beware of false prophets. They come to *you* in sheep's clothing, but inwardly they are ravenous wolves ...by their fruits you will recognize them." The fruits are set up as criteria for truth and knowledge. Europe is to be judged by the criteria it has set for itself.

In the preface to the *Wretched of the Earth* by Fanon, Jean-Paul Sartre, a French European says, "our victims know us by their wounds and shackles: that is what makes their testimony irrefutable. They only need to know what we have done to them for us to realize what we have done to ourselves."[4] European democracy has been compatible with the European colonization of Africans; it has been compatible with neocolonialism and apartheid, and it has been compatible with racism. If one bears in mind that democratic Europe has been and is a Christian Europe, European Christianity has been compatible with these afflictions of Africans. Moreover, under the aegis of European democracy and European Christianity, law and ethics have orchestrated these afflictions. To Africans, European democracy and European Christianity have amounted to the cultivation tyrants. It is not a surprise that generally, today, in Africa what passes as democracy, law, or ethics is indistinguishable from tyranny. Most African leaders, as is the case with most African states profess to be democratic. They all profess to be for the people. The law and the ethics they promulgate are a part of this profession. They dare not call themselves tyrannical. But it is not a secret that from the standpoint of the "fruits" criteria, they are ravenous wolves in sheep's clothing. Without shame, political leaders flock into the churches or into to other places of worship and never hesitate to align themselves with religious institutions to legitimize themselves.

Ravenous wolves in sheep's clothing can be at home wherever one finds human beings. As postcolonial Africa has demonstrated, there is a place for them in Africa. Africa accommodates them. It is facile and mystifying to blame Europeans or other people for their existence. In Africa too, ravenous wolves in sheep's clothing are known by their fruits. It is indeed true that some of the clothing has been imported from Europe: democracy, law, and ethics. The importation has the same implications called to our attention by Nietzsche. The strongest evidence comes from the daily lives of the masses of Africans. The empty rhetoric of democracy, law, and ethics barely seeks to whitewash the tyranny to which the masses are subjected daily. Ultimately, it is the sense of dignity of being African that is debased.

If what is said above is taken to heart, the inevitable conclusion is a form of practice – the practice of removing the ravenous wolves' covering. The removal renders the African naked. Yes, the African must walk naked, see himself or herself as such, and be seen by others as such. For others to see them as such, they too must walk naked and be seen by Africans as such. Nakedness does not breed shame. It brings light to the truth of our being. To be human, all human beings stand naked in the face of each other. This is a fundamental teaching of African African legal ethics and, indeed, of every other legal ethics. Ultimately, it is what law and ethics are about.

When Ortega y Gasset points out that man is a novelist of himself, by "man" he is not referring to "an individual" – the mainstay of modern European liberal anthropology – lone individuals who exist in isolation from other individual human beings. He also does not have in mind a Kantian individual. He is our spokesperson – speaking on behalf of all of us – not only collectively but also communally. If this is what he has in mind, he expresses half the truth of being human. As pointed out in *Ubuntu*, no individual is fully human without membership of the organic human community that makes him or her be what he or she is.

Legal ethics is an ethics on being human. As such, it is not subject to a substantive conclusion. A substantive conclusion can only be the end of humankind. Till then, being human will inevitably be ahead of itself. Legal ethics must be tailored accordingly. It ends where it begins and begins where it ends. It resides where it is: between its beginning and its end and between its end and its beginning. It resides where it begins and where it ends.

The French philosopher, Maurice Merleau-Ponty once observed,

> Whatever one's philosophical or even theological position, a society is not the temple of value-idols that figure on the front of its monuments or in its constitutional scrolls; the value of a society is the value it places upon man's relation to man ... To understand and to judge a society, one has to penetrate its basic structure to the human bond upon which it is built: this undoubtedly depends upon legal relations, but also upon forms of labor, ways of loving, living, and dying.[5]

The conclusion of what has been said about African African legal ethics compels one to come face to face with oneself. It is on oneself that this ethics is inscribed. Looking at oneself is not looking away from other human beings. It is in relation to them that one is what one is. There is a popular African proverb that says, "It takes a village to raise a child." When a child becomes an adult he or she does not move away from the village. He or she is an adult of the village. One does not get away from one's cradle. A village is a human village. It is a cradle of humanity. A human being is always a human being. He or she does not mutate into a stone.

Legal ethics whether African or non-African, is a mirror of the present life, but it is a present life that is pregnant with a future life. It is actual as well as ideal. It must be constantly birthed. The world of African African legal ethics remains to be created. In creating it, Africans are joined and must be joined by fellow human beings. It is a creative human pro-ject, – a pro-ject in which human beings create who or what they are. Uniting law and ethics or recognizing the unity of law and ethics energizes and vitalizes this creative pro-ject. Legal ethics is an invitation extended to all of us by all of us under-take this human pro-ject.

A hand, however big, can never cover the sky

An African proverb

Notes

1 Strauss shares a deeply ingrained error about Greek thought – the error in believing that Greek thought is sui generis. The historical fact is that Greek thought was in part influenced by non-Greek thought, more particularly, by African-Egyptian thought. See Professor Christos C. Evangeliou's book, *The Genesis of Philosophy When Greece Met Africa.* Sioux City, IA: Parnassos Press, 2015.
2 Frantz Fanon, The Wretched of the Earth, trans. Richard Philcox. New York: Grove Press, 2004, p. 150.
3 Fredrich Nietzsche, *Beyond Good and Evil*, trans. Walt Kaufmann. New York: Random House (Vintage), p. 177.
4 Frantz Fanon, The Wretched of the Earth, p. xlviii.
5 Maurice Merleau-Ponty, *Humanism and Terror*, trans. John O'Neil. Boston. MA: Beacon Press, 1969, p. xiv.

Index

For Product Safety Concerns and Information please contact our EU
representative GPSR@taylorandfrancis.com
Taylor & Francis Verlag GmbH, Kaufingerstraße 24, 80331 München, Germany

www.ingramcontent.com/pod-product-compliance
Ingram Content Group UK Ltd.
Pitfield, Milton Keynes, MK11 3LW, UK
UKHW022028061126
477531UK00003B/99
9780367427085